6422   6/-

Edgar Wright

with love from Auntie Jane

Oct. 6th 1942.

THE STRIDING DALES

KILNSEY WITH ITS MASSIVE, SPHINX-LIKE CRAG

The Striding Dales

THE
STRIDING DALES

BY

HALLIWELL SUTCLIFFE

WITH FRONTISPIECE IN COLOUR
AND SEVENTY-FOUR LINE ILLUSTRATIONS

BY

A. REGINALD SMITH, R.W.S.

FREDERICK WARNE & CO., LTD.
LONDON AND NEW YORK

Printed in Great Britain

FOREWORD

THE Yorkshire highlands, raking up to wide-flung mountain fastnesses, lie remote from usual haunts; and their people are rooted in free, unspoiled acres. There is only the one road to knowledge of the Dales and Dalesfolk —lifelong intimacy with the rugged scarps, the hidden glens, the homesteads, big and little, perched on the mountains' feet or gathered into grey, comely villages. Here and there a market town is busy with agriculture's pleasant merchandise. Never are men far from the overwatching moors, whose minstrels are plover and curlew, grouse and hoarse hoodie-crow.

Land and people have grown into a sure, ripe communion, and to be admitted to their fellowship is to learn the deeper things that reach the true romance. Legend and history mingle with the everyday of human intercourse. Storm and shine, the nor'-easter's bite on sleety uplands, the fragrance of swathed hayfields when summer dusks steal down about a land of plenty, the gypsies' caravans, slow-winding through a country friendly to them from the ancient days—who shall tell what goes to the Dales' full glamour?

I do not care to ask, but count myself favoured to have shared for a lifetime the rich measure of their friendship. I am happy, too, in another comradeship. By old habit, whenever I despair of words as a medium for expressing colour, I seek out my collaborator, and browse among his drawings. With a charmed brush in his hands he goes into our highlands and our dells, and captures the infinite, beguiling magic of form and colour in Dales that do not yield their secrets lightly. A flock of grey sheep, meandering between grey limestone walls, becomes a poem of many subtle undertones. The purple of snow-clad heights, the kindly hues of lichened roofs, all come at his bidding to canvases that are instinct with the very spirit of the uplands.

CONTENTS

CONTENTS

CONTENTS

ILLUSTRATIONS IN TEXT

ILLUSTRATIONS IN TEXT

THE STRIDING DALES

I

BOLTON PRIORY

Bolton Bridge—The Vision Splendid—The Marauders from the North—The Emissaries of King Henry—A local Proverb.

BOLTON BRIDGE sweeps in a comely arch across Wharfe River, brown with moorland peat; and the road goes forward, after its long stride, between quiet pastures where the cattle graze. There is nothing to suggest the nearness of a world's corner left to brood over mediæval dreams and listen to the chants of monks —chants broken not seldom by the clamour of marauding Scots—until the old tithe-barn lifts its slant roof to the sky. A gallant barn—perhaps the biggest in the North, and certainly the shapeliest—it bulges no longer with grain from Priory fields, but it remembers far-off harvests.

From the barn, onward to the outer wall of the Priory, there is constantly the sense of remembrance, blowing round one like a keen, yet fragile air. The dead outnumber the living always, and they are mighty here at Bolton.

This outer wall, with gillyflowers creviced everywhere between its stones, must have offered once a stout barrier against intrusion; and, as one passes through its gap, heart and mind are stilled for a moment. Many painters have brought their genius to this place of a thousand memories. Enthralled by love of Priory and forest-lands and the over-watching hills, they bring a great picture to birth once every while; but always they have the most divine discontent with the finished canvas.

In winter snow and spring-time glamour, in mid-June heat, in the ripe wonderland of glory that October brings to this

The pensive charm of Bolton

hard-bitten northland, great souls have come to Bolton, thinking to capture her beauty once for all. How could they hope to do it, when the Priory has weathered centuries of happenings, and broods about her memories with a still and jealous reticence? Poets have come here, too, and masters of vivid prose have done their best and mourned that it was so little, after all. They have tried to paint in words all that Bolton means, and she eludes such efforts.

There are ampler ruins of the kind, abbeys and priories with more to give the antiquaries. But there is none like Bolton. The grace of her, the pensive charm, are bosomed in a wonderland that could happen nowhere else. In front are the sheep-cropped grass lands, the mellow sunlight spinning rainbow gossamer from autumn leaves. To the right, Wharfe River flows like a strong, encircling arm and croons a lullaby to times that are over and gone. Behind and above the peace are the rough-hewn hills, the forest trees ablaze with autumn's leafage.

It is these hills beyond that make of Bolton, not a lost shrine where men and women worshipped in vague, far-off days, but a living presence. The over-guarding moors have known drought in summer, when grouse came to their drinking-pools and found them empty. They have known the way of skelping winds that brought the snows and made rise and hollow one level waste of white and bitter cold. Age after age, they have looked down on the Priory in its prosperous times. They saw its foundations laid, watched its walls grow a little and a little higher, till there came a day when the sun got up above these rugged moors, and wiped the mists away, and showed them the vision splendid, there in the valley. Bolton Priory had grown to its full height, as a child grows to a woman's quiet and comely dignity. And ever afterwards the hills doted on this daughter of their own, and watched, and were glad and sorry with her, every day and every year that saw her life-struggle.

They listened to matin bell and vesper call, chiming low and silvery up the slopes. They watched the acres prosper like a story of old Palestine—sheep grazing in a land of plenty, and cattle sleepy with the rich cud they  chewed. They saw great folk arrive—bishops and kings, and hunting-parties of the gentry, benighted after roaming far afield. There was nothing the hills missed, from their lodging near the skies, of all that happened to this child of their old age.

The prosperous years went by on tranquil feet. The needy and the maimed gathered thick about the Priory gate, and were not denied. Men outlawed and sore-pressed ran breathless in for sanctuary. They, too, were welcome, for Bolton, true to the faith that had built her, was all men's friend, and especially the sinners'. It was a life of sincerity, of busy happenings, of glamoured prayer and worship threading the meanest task.

In a land of plenty

By day the Prior and his household had the sunlight glinting on Wharfe River and up the grassy slopes. By night the stars wheeled up to guard them, quiet sentries of the sky, and owls made music for them in the woods. Some had been hunting, or fishing for the Friday's fast. Some had been praying, others chopping wood or milling flour. It did not matter what the errand. All was consecrate, and deep in their hearts they knew it, so that the spring of all their doings welled upward from some hidden fount of benison and courage. Perhaps their lives were drifting into a content too great, an ease too softening. There was peril from within, maybe, lest the full glow of praise and worship staled. So the lesser evil came—peril, dire and urgent, from without.

4

The hills looked down one summer's day on the wood-smoke curling from the Priory's kitchen, on men going about their usual affairs. They heard belfry chimes threading the vale below with silver-throated peace. Then from the northern track a sterner music sounded—wolf-cries of the Scots who had broken over the Border and come down in search of spoil. They found it, rich and ready. The gentle wall that Bolton Priory had reared against intrusion was breached in a score places. They drove through and plundered where they willed, thrusting the Prior and his folk into shelter of the woods— and that night they bivouacked with the dead in Bolton's graveyard.

Next day the hills got out of troubled sleep—nightmared by memories of what had chanced—and sunrise, warming their grey, rugged heads, showed the Scots breakfasting in haste. Within the hour they had gone north again with their spoil, and the Priory was left desolate in a land of emptiness. But not for long. Through the summer's night the Prior and his folk had gone from farmstead to farmstead scattered up the fells, and now they brought sturdy pike and bow men, yeomen mounted for the fight—swineherds from the forest, too, and shepherds, and lusty vagrants travelling the roads. So the Prior set one and all to work. The wall breached in eight places was repaired; and before nightfall of this long, hot day they had put other work in train—that of adding height and thickness to the wall.

Day after day the hills watched willing labour build, not a slender barrier, but a rampart, against the next invasion; and they took heart again, seeing their daughter in the safe hands of a Prior given to avenge or defend her honour. If peace, and sanctuary in which to worship were only to be gained by battle— well, battle it must be.

The years went by, broken by fight and bloody skirmishes

when the Scots came down, over and over again. If the Priory suffered hurt, its inmates repaired her walls, and afterwards went about their proper work of worship and land-tilling and succouring of the beggars at their gate. And never once, through centuries of hazard, did the parish priest—he who served the church within the Priory that was free to all the countryside—fail to take service there.

The prosperous years went by

Then once again the hills were grief-stricken. No Scots came marauding, but instead a retinue of horsemen, headed by a grave-faced man who seemed to have little relish for his errand, drew rein at the Prior's gate. The Prior was there to greet him, at the head of the company that was saying farewell to all it loved. Their sorrow bit so deep that they disdained to show it, and out of this hardy stillness came something that increased the horseman's gravity.

" The King asks for your keys, Prior," he said.

" They are here. And now, by your leave, give room to us."

As if he were a conqueror, the Prior claimed right of way. The emissaries of King Henry reined aside, and between them went a sober company. There was no falter in their steps, until they met the beggar men, the lame and sick, who clustered round the outer gate. They were aware suddenly how these pensioners had grown into their lives.

" Is it true ? " shrilled a beggar woman.

" Sadly true, daughter," said the Prior gently, and halted to give a last blessing, and passed on—out into the wilderness, firm of step and courage.

The roofless Priory, backed by the russet of October hills, once in a long while shows this quick vision of the centuries— shows it as though a day were short as a heart-beat, and a year like the passing of a moment. Such visions are apt to ring true; for history is told, not in books only, but in the silences that wait for every man in every corner of our storied Dales.

If you would take courage in both hands, and cease to be a mourner for brave days over and done with, choose the hour between sundown and the murk of dusk, and roam with a quiet heart among the Priory ruins. You may hear the water-wheel going *rub-a-dub-dub* again as it grinds the garnered corn. Big-throated chants of praise may take you unawares, and far-off cries of shepherds to their dogs, though all modern sheep are folded safe and their guardians snug indoors.

If still your heart is quiet and unafraid, listen on. The church that served all and sundry of the countryside is roofed for worship still, and in this quiet hour its continuity of service comes round one like a benediction. The ruined masonry surrounding Bolton's little parish church takes on a new significance. Death has not claimed the Priory. Her spirit, warm and glowing, watches over this enchanted corner of the world.

It is easy, at such an hour and in such a place, to understand a proverb rife once on a time among the local shepherds : " All lands are thrifty that look down on Bolton Priory." A fine, happy truth such as should come from men whose work lies on the uplands, where sky and loneliness are near at all times. They are more guarded nowadays ; yet now and then a hint is given that, on still evenings, while they go about their flocks, the echo of a vesper-bell steals up into the crannies of the fells. Could it be otherwise ?

II

SKIPTON-IN-CRAVEN

Skipton Castle—The Splendid Cliffords—The Shepherd Earl—A Great Lady—Barden Gap.

TO know the full story of Bolton Priory, one must needs begin with the good town of Skipton-in-Craven. And that is no hardship. To come up the High Street on a summer's morning, with the Castle gateway and its grim motto "*Désormais*" carved in stone—to see the long, grey Church that stands beside it, so that both seem one in dignity and strength—is to feel the pulse quicken and the step grow light. Here, too, the past dwarfs the present and is paramount. To right and left, piercing the houses and the shops, are narrow entries, opening into courtyards clustered thick with dwellings. One wonders nowadays why men chose to live in quarters so shut out from sunlight of the open street. It was because the Scots came raiding. These entries could be barred readily against intrusion, making each courtyard a little fortress of its own; and there was bitter need of it in Skipton's tale of doings.

FitzDuncan—nephew of the King of Scots—came raiding here when the twelfth century was young. He sacked the Castle and went north again, driving his spoil of cattle and weeping women before him. Fourteen years later he remembered how fat these lands of Craven were, and came again. This time he not only sacked the Castle, but found there the Lady Adeliza—a child at his first coming, but now in the hey-day of her beauty. Romance found the weak joints in his armour.

9

What he had won by the sword he claimed afresh by marriage with Skipton's heiress ; and from that marriage sprang the boy whose death, so legend says, gave Bolton Priory to the world. Skipton was a storm centre always for many kinds of struggle, and legend and history alike have much to tell of Scottish raids. In the Gargrave country, not far away, nine churches are rumoured to have stood where now only one remains. This is not history of the kind supported by documents, but a tale passed down faithfully by yeoman fathers to their sons.

Persistently the brief tale survives. There were nine churches, serving a wide-flung populace of farmer-folk and gentry. And one night a beacon flared in warning that the Scots would reach them on the morrow. The gentry got their serving-men together, the farmers their hinds. Few were too weak or old to accept the venture. They met the enemy at an outlet of the hill-road known to this day as Scots Gap, and put up such a battle against odds that not one of them returned. The raiders passed on to pillage of the churches, and were about to raze the last of the nine when a company rode from Skipton Castle and put them to the rout.

Such happenings were built into Skipton's past. Is it strange that she stirs now and then in her prosperous ease and remembers other days ? It would be stranger if memories failed to wake. With age-old towns, as with men, there are times when ancestry leaps out ; and they stand in the thick of passions that were not buried with their dead. There is an hour of this sort comes to Skipton every while, when dawn is astir before the sleepy chimneys wake for the day's routine. She thrills with presage of happenings to come. A little breeze flutes in and out, and then grows still. The throstle piping his daybreak song somewhere among the churchyard trees forgets to sing. A hushed silence gathers, waiting for the dead who live.

Far down the spacious High Street comes the tramp of feet.

A trumpet challenges the red, forth-riding dawn. Horses neigh in shrill reply. And suddenly the street is packed with wayfarers. He who held Skipton Castle for the Norman King rides first, proud and lusty, a conqueror. His gentry, close

Skipton-in-Craven

behind, laugh at the wild plaudits of the crowd. A man full of sores obtrudes himself and plucks at the leader's bridle.

"Nay, I'm not Royalty, to heal you of King's Evil," says De Meschines gently, and puts money into his hand, and rides on.

He halts for a moment at the Castle gateway, salutes its carven motto of "*Désormais*," but cannot stay for bite or sup as when the blood was red in him. He and his pass on, grey phantoms now against the ardent dawn.

Behind them, in close following, ride the next heirs to Skipton's pride. The High Street is one endless, swaying line of horsemen, men on foot, women fluttering kerchiefs from windows overhead. The splendid Cliffords pass, inheritors of Skipton's honour—the Sailor Earl—the Shepherd Earl, reared on lone Cumbrian heights until war ceased between the roses of York and Lancaster. Many another of the line halts to salute the Castle gateway, and is gone, winding up the steep road to Embsay and the further heights.

For all the Cliffords' splendour, there are gaps between their progress up the High Street. The crowd lining every foot of space ceases its heedless cheers, as Christopher Aske comes up the street, with space behind him and in front. In the dark of night he went alone, except for the Vicar of Skipton and two others, and rescued the Castle's ladies, in sanctuary at Bolton Priory, from foul dishonour of the mob. Kerchiefs do not wave only now. They are dropped from every window that he passes. And Aske thanks them with a smile bright as polished armour, and rides forward.

Another Clifford comes, full-fed with panoply and self-importance. The sweating populace cheers, its throat grown hoarse by this time. Again a space is kept, and again the uproar dies. Into that silence steps Kit Norton, not heeding aught but his great love of Mary, Queen of Scots. She goes with him, gracious beyond his dreams of her in days gone by. She had only known him then as a pleasant youth who fell victim to her charm and rescued her from prison for a brief two hours. Yet through the captive years that followed, her thoughts must have returned often to that evening when, at Bolton in Yoredale, Kit Norton planned the great escape. She must have recalled their breathless ride together, the end of it, her tragic turning to him as the Castle soldiery thundered down in hot pursuit.

" Am I always to lure men to death ? "

" No," he answered simply—" to life."

The great dream had been his. It is with him now, as he goes up the High Street. Whatever country he returns from, love of the Queen abides with him, triumphant and secure.

Another Clifford passes up the street, insolent in pride and well-being, till on the sudden a galloping horseman swirls down the Raikes, and over the ford, and reins up sharply on the edge of the cheering throng.

Skipton Market

" The Scots are coming ! " he cries, between harsh, panting breaths.

In a moment the mob is running hard for safety, each man jostling his neighbour for right of entry through the narrow gateways of their closes. The Clifford, alone with his company of knights and men-at-arms, turns with quiet disdain.

" The Scots are coming ? Let them come."

" They're in strength, my lord."

" So is Skipton Castle, friend."

" They're lusty with the thought of Bannockburn. They come in strength, I say."

With that he gets to the gallop again and rackets down the

emptied street to pass the warning forward. Clifford and his folk cross the drawbridge and prepare for a siege not long delayed.

At dawn next day the watchers on the battlement hear a far-off murmur on the northern road—a murmur that swells presently to stormy uproar—and down the Raikes comes pouring what seems an endless line of warriors. The Scots are here, in strength. The siege is sharp and eager. Used to the taking of strongholds dour and stubborn in defence, they make short work of the attack ; and where the watchmen stood not long since, smoke and flame lick round the battlements.

The tumult lessens and dies slowly out to silence. The Scots have gone north again with their spoil. And presently the street rings to a new uproar, as the masons set about re-building gaping walls.

Then, with scarcely a break in this pageant that floods Skipton's High Street, come other Cliffords with their retinues, in idle, merrymaking pomp—until one rides between silent, awe-struck crowds that give no plaudits, but blessings drenched with tears.

The Shepherd Earl, his peace-days changed for war's, leads a great company of Dalesmen to the fight that is afterwards to be known as Flodden Field. Gentry and yeomen on horseback, lusty farmers and their lads on foot, move quietly up the street, and round the road-bend, and out to the silence that means days and nights of mortal anguish for their women-folk. In the men's faces is only grim remembrance of what the Scots have done to Skipton and the Dales for centuries—only the will and heart to put an end to such intrusions for all time.

They pass, and the street is full suddenly of men in leather helmets and half-armour, attacking in useless force the gateway with its frowning, stone-cut challenge of "*Désormais.*" And now again the drawbridge drops and clangs, and Sir John Mallory, the Castle's governor, rides out with all his men.

Surrender, at the end of three years' siege, is forced on him; but he yields on his own terms. To look at this lean, famine-stricken garrison, you would think them conquerors. They are armed. Their banners are still their own, to meet the free breeze from the moors above, and in their faces is the light that knows no counterfeit.

And after that is silence, till a roomy carriage, drawn by a team of greys, has all the High Street to itself. Out of it steps

Straight and wide the High Street strides to the church that is a true Cathedral

Lady Anne Clifford, last of her race—and greatest, except for the Shepherd Earl, her ancestor. She has come, whether the Protector likes it or no, to rebuild the Castle's shattered walls, as her folk reared them afresh after onset of the Scots. A great lady—great of heart and mind and courage—she gets the masons to work, watches the task go forward, then takes her stately way to Barden, to rebuild there the Hunting Tower beloved of the Shepherd Earl before and after he took his Dalesmen up to Flodden Field.

Our way is Lady Anne Clifford's, up the Bailey, past the Castle wall, and out to Barden; but there is time to halt for deeper acquaintance with the gallant spaciousness that makes Skipton-in-Craven like no other in a land rich with ancient towns. Straight and wide the High Street strides to the church that is a true Cathedral. Its grey, long front merges into the Norman gateway of the Castle. Both are linked inseparably with the long line of Cliffords.

Within the church, on either side of the steps leading to the High Altar, stand the Clifford tombs. One of the two is simple in its dignity. The other is almost barbaric in its pride of race. Shield after painted shield shows marriages of the race with daughters of the Throne or of those near its glamour. The Cliffords were ever half-royal, free spenders and keen fighters. Regents for the southern King in our hard-bitten North, they prospered and deceased ; but their church remains, and the Norman keep that flings its challenge of " *Désormais* " to the sky.

Eager dawn lies over Skipton Town as we turn at last to take the Barden Road. We encounter no traffic of modern flesh-and-blood ; but presently we overtake the living pageantry that not long ago swept through Skipton's spacious street. Every Clifford of them all has lingered, rejoicing in the fell lands known of yore. Christopher Aske has checked his stride. That other Christopher, bred of the Rylstone Nortons, is with them. The sun climbs higher as we go through Embsay village, and up past Eastby's grey hamlet. Phantoms of the lesser sort are compelled, they say, to dwindle into emptiness at cock-crow ; but these stalwarts of the elder days are bound by no such rule. They journey with us up the sandy road, between the heather and the brackens, till we come to Barden Gap.

A moment since we were in Airedale. A stride takes us to the Vale of Wharfe. The whole virile, eager land seems to leap at us with wide-flung eagerness. Away to the left, Whernside and Buckden Pike and Arncliffe Clouder are outposts of the higher Dale. Ahead, the fells straddle the far wastes of Greenhow, where the lonely acres lie shelterless to winter gales and August's torrid heat. Bluff Simon's Seat surveys his kingdom of the heights. To the right, long fells reach down to the favoured haven where Bolton Priory stands fragrant in her desolation. Her litanies, recited through the centuries, her songs of praise, the music of her bells, are real, here at Barden Gap, as the great-hearted phantoms that led one up the track; and all the yesterdays lie close in wait for travellers.

III

MONASTIC DAYS

A Fatal Leap—The Gentlemen Free-lances of the Priory—The Jolly Waggoners—An Old-Style Tale—A Place Set Apart.

FITZDUNCAN and Adeliza, heiress of Skipton, had one son only, the Boy of Egremonde. As soon as he could sit a horse, the lad must have ridden up this track that strides so sharply through Barden Gap. Down in Wharfedale yonder the Barden forests and the pasture lands, rich in game, were a great hunting ground for the Lords of Skipton, whether they coursed the stag or loosed their falcons on lesser prey. The boy must have learned early, too, the perilous joy of the leap across the Strid, where Wharfe's full-bosomed stream narrows and frets between deep walls of rock. And there came a day when he tried to cross with a hound in leash. The hound checked and faltered, dragging him to his death in the swift torrent ; and that night a woe-begone retainer sought audience of the Lady Adeliza, and told his tale.

Legend tells how she came through that fire of grief. The quiet, compelling beauty of Bolton Priory, in its ruins, is eloquent of the mother's struggle from midnight to the further dawn. Out of her anguish rose, as from a grave, a song made manifest in stone. The hills were kindly with it. Wharfe River folded it in close embrace. From the beginning this Priory was given a soul, tender, strong, persuasive. The mortar of its stones was mixed, not with water only, but with human tears, and set the better for it. No legend of the Dales has found deeper and more lasting roothold. It will survive and flower anew down succeeding generations, for as long as northern hearts beat true to the blended pathos and courage that are instinct in the simple tale.

Where Wharfe's full-bosomed stream narrows and
frets between deep walls of rock

The house prospered, and took a peculiar place in the history of monastic times. Its discipline, though never lax or slipshod, was not austere. Its worship was simple and devout, its love of the best in this life healthy as its hope in the hereafter. Tragedies there were, of course. No company as big as Bolton's could lack its backsliders. But the Priory's tale goes on from century to century with the same spacious, happy atmosphere, disturbed only by incursions of the Scots. These onslaughts were harassing enough, and grew so frequent at one period that Scottish visits might be looked for oftener than the Bishop's. Time after time the Prior and all his people were driven to the woods, while the enemy sacked and looted as they willed.

Then in self-defence a company of gentry was added to the Prior's household. Scions of great Yorkshire families, they were skilled in war, and brought to Bolton's cloistered quiet, no doubt, all the devil-may-care high spirit that is apt to be the sole portion of younger sons. They found good, rough material ready to their hand for training a soldiery to meet the Scots. The Priory lands were cropped by countless sheep and cattle, swine and goats and geese. The serfs attending these had learned skill in archery by bitter need. Wolves and wild boars had their lairs in forests where the swine roamed in search of beech-nuts ; and swine-tending was no sinecure in those days.

Out of these hardy Northmen—who could sleep peacefully on a bed of acorns with a wet wind blowing through the forest across their guardian fire of cones and deadwood—the gentlemen free-lances of the Priory built a company, so sharp in attack, so stubborn in defence, that the Scots learned a superstitious dread of plundering Church lands in these parts. Their visits were paid at longer and at longer intervals, till they ceased altogether.

Toll of another kind, however, was levied on the Priory. The Bishop—usually a keen out-of-doors man and a hunter— found increasing zest in visitations to this good country where deer and game of all kinds were abundant. The Prior kept a good table, too, and his gentlemen-at-arms were excellent company. The Bishop was apt to bring a party of two or three hundred with him on these sporting visitations, and the Prior, on one occasion at least, is known to have murmured, after bidding his visitors farewell, " The Scots were cheaper

guests." That is one note of Bolton's history—humour, dry
and quiet. Prayer is another, sincere, devout. Work and play
fill up the days and years in true proportion.

Looking down the centuries, whose tale is known to us in
detail intimate as a household book of facts and figures, we see
a world of well-worth-while—a real world, such as they make a
pageant of in these days. There was no pageantry about the

" Come, and welcome to you, friend "

Middle Ages. Those who were privileged to live then were
downright folk, living their lives in the open. Peril was real—
from wild beasts and attack of human foes. Work for daily
bread was real. So was the call to prayer when, across the
darkening twilight, lost wayfarers heard the Priory bell ring out
its " Come, and welcome to you, friend." Prelate or thief,
tinker or travelling packman, was sure of a night's lodging here
at Bolton. It was, indeed, a great tavern of the Dale, and of
wider England ; and its provisioning was a matter of ceaseless

urgency and care. Venison and other meats, of bird and beast, were to be had in abundance within its own borders. They grew and milled corn for bread. Wharfe River brought fish to its threshold, and the Cellarer was skilled in brewing ale of many strengths, from nut-brown " milk for hinds " to the deep-coloured " Old October " that was potent as a battle song.

But wine they could not make, and for that they had to send great waggons to the port of Hull. Two thousand gallons of French and Spanish wines seems a monstrous allowance for one year, till one remembers that the Priory's fixed establishment—monks, lay-brethren, gentlemen-at-arms, cooks and millers and swineherds—numbered two hundred. Pilgrims, journeying from shrine to shrine, were frequent. Not only benighted companies of gentry, but Royalty, called here for entertainment, and wine flowed at these times like Wharfe in spate. It is surprising, indeed, that they took so small a toll from Spain and France for the needs of their guest tables, apart from their own needs. Sugar they could not make, nor spices to flavour many a gallant dish. For these they sent to Boston, with its church tower looking seaward across the marshy flats of Lincolnshire.

Always there's the coming in to Bolton of travellers from afar, and always the out-journeys of waggoners who go from the Priory to the world beyond its borders. Boston is not far away from Hull, and a vivid picture leaps to mind of those waggons joining company on the northern road. Loaded with sugar and spices, some, and more with the kegs of wine known as doliums, they would jolt and creak their way to sequestered Bolton. The blue sky over them, and the wild-rose thickets at the roadside, would hear rough, cheery banter of the waggoners, homing for the Priory and its wealth of cheer.

In my dreams I plan an old-style tale, its whole action taking place on the road between Hull and Bolton. The names alone of the farm-servants at the Priory invite one to a debauch of lusty comedy. What of Adam Blunder, Tom Noght, Jolyneddy, Richard Drunkur, Simon Paunche? The most felicitous invention could not better these names written on the Priory's roll-book, existent to this day. One would choose those five at once as waggoners, and send them straight into the journey north with their doliums of wine, their spices and their sugar. They would have diverting encounters on the road. Wayside taverns, where they halted for the night, would rock with laughter at their cantrips. Anything, in or out of reason, would be possible to stout fellows carrying such names as Jolyneddy and Simon Paunche. There would be ambushes in wait for them—rough, sturdy ambushes of prowlers who stuck at nothing—and these would be galloped through by Adam Blunder's vast simplicity, or Jolyneddy's guile. Or perhaps Richard Drunkur would find inspiration in his cups, and pilot the good waggons through.

These five, in the comedy that is dear to me as a man's dream-children always are, make a thrifty stir about the road to Bolton. They tumble into adversity for the love of getting out of it, at hazard. Their comments on those who live within the home-walls, from the Prior downward, are shrewd. And through this stirring tale, spring is enticing the plover home again from alien shores, and daffy-down-dillies curtsey to the breeze. Villagers, moreover, are bringing the hay home on loaded wains that brush the sweet of honeysuckle in the hedges ; and there's the memory-haunted reek of autumn fires, lit by foresters when they burn the " brash " of littered underwood.

Such a delectable blend of the seasons, of course, ought not to happen at one and the same time. But in dreams it not only can, but does. This tale of the road from Hull to Bolton has one singular advantage. It is gifted with the power to bring every flower that blooms from March to wild October, every joy of spring's light-footed frolic and summer's wide-eyed laughter, into the compass of one journey up to Bolton. The singing birds—thrush and lark, and blackbird sweet of throat—are a massed orchestra. And whenever they rest to dip their bills in near-by pools, the chaffinch lets his pipe be heard.

Through it all go my brave five with their wains. To carry doliums of wine up the Great Road should be enough for any man's delight in waggoning. The strong brine-stench lingers still about the barrels that have tasted the worst a sea crossing could do to them. And every company of vagabonds about the Road is bent on waylaying a treasure that would slake their thirst for many a month to come. Sundry of these rascals ply Richard Drunkur with ale at a convenient tavern, and he succumbs. But four are left. Then Simon Paunche yields to fierce temptation of a meal that would furnish a guest table for two lesser men. Only Jolyneddy and Adam Blunder and Tom Noght are left to carry forward. They do it blithely, after tucking Simon and Richard somewhere between the doliums and the hay-trusses that will feed the horses later on.

The waggons jog forward steadily, over flat country billowing to the sky. Golden cornfields bend to the wind. Pomp and penury meet them everywhere. In those days the North Road was never still. Knights and their ladies, hawks on wrist, were followed by grave merchants trafficking in wool. Men wounded in the French wars overseas came limping by, most of them too proud to ask for alms.

Through it all still go my five waggoners, two of them out of action for awhile and pillowed among the hay. The cavalcade, near dusk, comes to a gloomy wood of pines that borders the way on either side. And here a company of thirsty souls is gathered, pledged to capture the waggons and drink deep. They have set a barrier of tree-trunks across the road. The Priory men counter this by feigning panic. Deserting their merchandise, they lie hid in the underbrush until the footpads—

a hundred strong, I think—have broached and dealt with the first cask of wine, and are roaring wild songs up into the moonlit sky.

The three waggoners now run up and down the wood, with shouts and sharp commands, as if they were a band of the King's soldiery. So much noise they make, from so close at hand, that the revellers bend unsteady legs to flight; and up and down between the misty tree-boles the teamsters thwack them with their cudgels. When they return, they find Richard Drunkur thrusting his head out from the hay-trusses.

"Friends," says he, "I dreamed men were at the wine-barrels. So I woke to guard them for the Prior."

There's no end to the ventures that brought them, as with music, up the Great North Road, and afterwards through by-ways to their Priory. And they magnified their doings, as men will, when they supped royally that night, till the shepherds and the swine-tenders believed they were Paladins returned from a perilous crusade.

Hazard, close at home, still assailed the Priory at intervals. The Scottish visitations, if less frequent, were savage, till Flodden closed that chapter once for all. The gentlemen-at-arms became poor younger sons again, their occupation gone, and once more Bolton's story opened out to spaciousness, and hunting of the deer, and feeding of the poor.

A great-hearted story, this of Bolton's. Its life was full-blooded. So was its religion. Through it all you smell the clean wind of the forest, hear matins and vespers tune themselves to bustle and thrifty work of the everyday. It was a place set apart, fighting and praying in its struggle for the Grail—living its life between-whiles with healthy, human vigour. The moil of politics destroyed it, so men fancied; but it only seemed to pass. There's no death, but vivid life, where the River puts a wide arm about the Priory she loves.

IV

GREY BARDEN

The Roving Tracks—Wharfe's Bridges—Ghyll Beck—The Legend of Squire Ramsden—A Sanctuary of the Living Dead—The Moor's Song.

IT is hard to write of the country bordering Barden Tower, grey on wooded highlands overlooking Bolton Priory. One's love of it goes back so far along the years. Sunrise and dusk—weather golden, russet, grey—watched the long intimacy grow. Now it is a land of charm so proven, of mystery so deep, that pen-pictures seem of slight account.

Rough moorlands stride down to the pine forest, sombre and austere except in spring, when the larch-green wimples and curtseys on either side of the winding highway, and in autumn, when these same larches shed their leaves and strew a carpet of bright gold, soft for wayfaring feet to tread. Below, if a man leaves the road and takes the roving tracks that lead between the big-boled firs, he ventures into wonderland. The great silences are here, stirred by the small people's underfret—squirrels that seem to vanish at your coming till there's a movement overhead and you see a pair of bright eyes watching you between forked boughs—rabbits that tumble head-over-heels into their burrows —a stoat chattering in swift retreat.

Ring-doves croon together, and somewhere a woodpecker is tapping. The red brush of a fox slips shadow-like away from your intrusion. If you come by night, and the moon is up, you may hear a music scarcely louder than the forest's silence. You

follow it, taking care to crack no fallen twig, till you find yourself in a clearing where foxgloves nod between the lichened tree-
stumps. You are aware that unseen elves, disturbed at play,
are watching you. Soft, Puck-like laughter seems to rustle
through the hollow, blending with the Green Folk's forest-song
that gets into your heart. You are rapt away into the kingdom
of worth-while, and the years of your human vagabondage show
only the silver lights and golden.

Barden Tower, grey on wooded highlands

Elves' Hollow left behind, the track winds steeply down.
The majestic silence of the forest is broken by a close and
swelling murmur that grows soon to the night-song of Wharfe
River as she swirls to the arches of Barden Brigg. Bridges
stand strong and silent. It is their business to let prince and
beggarman, priest and waggoner's wain, go safe from bank to
bank; but the River is a thing of motion, talking as she goes.

To-night Wharfe tells of Oughtershaw, far-off among the fells
where the little rills that were her childhood gathered from lone
mountain slopes. She tells of Hubberholme, where Hubba the
Dane raided, and settled, and built the most prayerful kirk in

all the Dale—of Kettlewell, and Coniston, and many a storied farmstead that hugs her banks.

Before ever a Roman legion trod the Dale, Wharfe was old and wise. After their time she heard the Scandinavian tongue, the Saxon and the Norman, and the modern Dalesman's speech that has garnered from them all. She has gathered the centuries' changes into her life hour by hour, year by year, and is the same counsellor to-day that she was to the Briton of a misty, far-off age. Love and hate, men's passion for tillage and their lust for war that tramples down the crops—jealousy, slinking like Reynard through the forest brakes—she has found them vary little as the world grows older. The same tempests roar from the hills. At such times Wharfe, wise and quiet and even-flowing, is startled by her own headlong fury, now as of old. The peat-red waters race and spume. Wherever limestone bluffs resist her, she snarls at them as she goes by, and snatches a bigger toll of sheep and cattle from the lands below, to spite the cliffs.

At usual times the bridges—how many of them, and how comely, down the Dale's grey length—are her friends, trusty and well-beloved, grave sentries at attention always to carry travellers across the waters. In these mad bursts of passion, Wharfe rives trees from her banks, to use as battering-rams. Once she broke every bridge from Oughtershaw to Bolton, except two; and those wise in old-time lore say that she cried and sorrowed for a year about their ruined buttresses till men built them up again. These poetic elders tell us that, of all the bridges who woo her to stay as she hurries by and be their mate, she loves only Barden. That is why nowadays you hear always, when the floods are still, a soft fare-well from Wharfe as she runs beneath the arches. She would stay if she might; but the lowlands draw her down. Perhaps it is this lover's heart of hers for Barden that bids her gem her banks just here with spendthrift bloom as spring strides into summer.

Suppose you have lingered so far into the short summer's night, letting Wharfe lay spells on you, that dawn-crimson and the moon are in the sky together. It is well to have stayed for such beguilement. The river's wide, unhurried flow mirrors a never-ceasing change of colour—rose and grey and eager blue— and through the pulsing woof and weft of the sky's reflected pattern the paling moon looks up from the stream's quiet depths. The forest stirs in its sleep. Little murmurs creep among the brackens and in branches stirred by the first, soft breeze of day. Blackbirds call sharply from a hazel-clump on the right. A cock crows lustily from some Barden farm. Another answers him across the valley. Dogs here and there begin to challenge Chanticleer's assumption that he is over-lord of this good country. Curlews cry fitfully, half-awake, above the tree-tops. A heron clouds the whole breadth of Wharfe for a moment, then glances down to the water and begins his fishing.

Day is up in the forest. Though you turn for home and the highway up above, your step is a laggard's. You are afraid to miss one chorister's note in the teeming litany that rises to the sun-glow and the thrifty warmth. Frail mists run fleecy through the undergrowth. And Wharfe River—comrade of the night and day—sends up her own anthem to summer and the hay-winning that soon will be astir in Barden's meadows. Little is changed since the days when Bolton Priory was reared, and the Cliffords built five hunting-towers in a country where their deer roamed wide and free.

As one follows the slanting, upward track, another murmur of waters sounds, and one comes suddenly on Ghyll Beck as it steps down to join the river. Enchantment is abroad again. Day may be eager to get about its work ; but all is out of sight, forgotten, except this moorland stream that has left the uplands for the woods. It comes with little sound, for its bed is one long stair of rock pools, brimming with gently-moving foam between their ferny brinks. Great beeches rear themselves on either bank, strong yet supple in their fresh young greenery ; and below them is the crimson of their last year's leaves, an undying flame that is fed afresh each autumn. Leaves eddy in the pools, and tinge their cool depths with living warmth. All things are believable as you go from step to step of its long stair, and up towards the moor.

Barden's Homestead

The din of circumstance, of ways and means, is stilled. Only real adventures meet you as you climb—a wood nymph, startled by the sound of human steps, halting where the briar roses grow —some hunter of the ancient days slaking a ghostly thirst at the stream—a shepherd-lad, come into this haunt of peace and understanding, to play sad tunes on his pipe, because grey-eyed Phyllis will have naught of him. As there are corners here and there about the Dale devised by nature to be sanctuaries for birds and squirrels and such small, defenceless people, so this ghyll is set apart for travellers returning from the elder day —the shapes of those who loved Barden so well in life that they cannot rest away from a homeland passionately dear.

You do not invoke them. They simply come to you, welcome and unbidden. No words, as such, reach your ears ; yet they have speech. It may be Squire Ramsden who comes from Appletreewick across the river—not dripping, for ghosts go dry-shod, as the saying is—and stands beside you. All that is legendary and vague about his one outstanding exploit grows strangely clear, as if four centuries were bridged and you watched his venture in the doing. He had been hunting the deer all day, had supped royally, and went to bed in great content. In the murkest of the night he stirred in his sleep, not wanting to, and heard a voice bidding him rise, to save more than life. The Squire turned over on his side with an ungentle oath, and slept. Again the voice summoned him, louder now, and still he would not budge.

" Bestir yourself, John Ramsden," said the voice, a third time. " If you be a man at all, bestir yourself."

So he got up unwillingly and went out on foot into the moonlight, thinking himself a fool for his pains as he dusted the sleep from his eyes. He went whither he was led, having no direction of his own—up the moon-white village street and out into the forest. Whenever the tracks branched, a voice whispered, " Choose this, and hasten." And he hurried on, still thinking himself daft to have got out of a warm bed to follow a boggart.

A white owl crossed his path. Its hunting note was harsh and eerie. Bats, too, were hawking their prey, and the underbrush was alive with twitterings and stealthy movements of he knew not what. The Squire had a stout heart for the forest's day-time perils, but these ghostly things of night were another matter. He felt strangely helpless. Yet he was drawn forward —faster and faster—till a cry rang sharply from beyond a clump of firs.

The Squire was running now. He came into a moonlit clearing, and in the middle of it saw a young maid struggling in the arms of a great, hulking fellow. Sir John had come without weapon of any sort except the brawny strength that was known at every wrestling match about the Dale. But the strength sufficed ; and, when he had done with the outlaw, the maid fainted in his arms. He knew then who had called to him across the night, whose voice it was that had whispered in his ear along the forest roads, guiding him. He knew, too, a wild tumult of the heart as he carried her over the clearing to her father's house. For he had loved her from afar for five whole years, thinking the Rose of the Dale cared nothing for him. And the end of it was marriage that, to the end, was courtship of each other, though they lived to see grandchildren clambering about their knees.

Sometimes a monk will come into this sanctuary of the Ghyll, sighing for the days when Bolton Priory was roofed, and peace and prayer were to be captured between marauding visits from the Scots—sighing for the nights when his brethren and he would come to Barden Tower and study star-lore with the Shepherd Earl from Skipton. And sometimes the Shepherd Earl himself—a rare and happy chance—returns to this old haunt, and sits by your side without ceremony. Born a Clifford—reared on hardship and the worst that north-country fells can do to their shepherds—brought suddenly to take his true place as over-lord of Skipton—he is a comrade like no other the Ghyll brings to one. Modest and gay, wise, buoyant with a pride not his only, but his forefathers', he brings one back to Flodden Field, tells just how they swirled, he and his lads of the Dale, into the stubborn battle. But his talk wanders soon from combat. It is of the forest and its deer now, of the stars whose wheeling courses through the sky he learned while tending sheep on the pastured roof-tops of our northern heights.

With him, into this sanctuary of the living dead, comes often Sylvester Lister, who carried a pike to Flodden under Clifford's leadership. The Listers, even at that day, had been settled for generations at Barden Tower. They are there still, their honour rooted deep in the Dale's tradition; and it is fitting that the pike Sylvester carried to the Border is guarded by the centuried walls of his old home.

There's no reason why one should ever leave this haunt of fellowship. Its people know no shams, and the free, full-blooded days of old return. Yet when one goes—up and up the rocky stair, with its nymph-pools brimming under guardian beeches—you find yourself still in a full-blooded country. For you stride up the broken lands and forward to the open moor. League on league the heather fares out to the sky. Not a tree or a shrub breaks its fine desolation. Gnarled and hummocky, bare and stalwart and unafraid, it is like the cock-grouse of its breeding—the grouse that stands on a boulder near at hand and challenges the world to come against him, because breeding-time and his mate are near. And this seems to be the burden of his challenge :

> " *I call to my mate from a boulder grey*
> *When stars grow dim at the peep of day,*
> *And I'm the King of the Heather.*
> *I ruffle my plumes, and I swell my throat,*
> *And, marry, there's strength in my harsh, queer note*
> *That's trained by the wind and the weather !*
> *Come back, come back, come back,*
> *Little wife, come you back, come back !*

> " *I challenge my foe from that boulder staunch,*
> *And the keen wind ruffles my sturdy paunch,*
> *While I'm the King of the Heather.*
> *My foe he drives with talon and beak*
> *Straight to the onset—I find him weak,*
> *And laugh with the wind and the weather.*
> *Come back, come back, come back,*
> *If you dare, come you back, come back !*

D

THE STRIDING DALES

" I call to my mate from a boulder grey,
When dusk creeps up to the Milky Way,
And I'm the King of the Heather.
I ruffle my plumes, and I swell my throat,
And, marry, there's strength in my harsh, queer note
That's blessed by the wind and the weather !
Come back, come back, come back,
Little wife, come you back, come back ! "

That is the moor's song, to-day as always. And, if you look closely, you may see a little man squatting beside you in the heather—little in height, if he were standing, but terribly broad and sinewy of body. His clothes are red-brown, like brackens when the autumn comes, and in his eyes is the slumbering light of feud. The forest and the heath—the two primæval things left us in a world of clamour—are still at odds. The Brown Man of the Moor sits waiting, his big head bunched on his shoulders. He loathes the forest for a lady-like thing that trips down to the softer lands and shakes her larch-tresses at him with disdain. He dreams of music soon to come—ring of the woodman's axe below, the rip and crash of falling beeches—and afterwards his free moor striding to the brink of Wharfe River and heather carpeting her rocks.

The moor's heart is strong and trusty. The forest's heart is sweet as a maid's. But the gulf of feud lies deep between the two.

V

THE WILD LANDS

*The Valley of Desolation—A Forest Romance—" Swart Simon"
—The Amanghams—The Greenhow Miners—The Ghostly Shift—
The Silver Spirit—The Road of the Lost—" Jannock "—The Freedom of
the Dale.*

IN all the fine diversity that is one of Wharfedale's attributes,
no change of scene, perhaps, is so abrupt as meets one just
beyond Bolton Priory and the Barden country. To stand
where Wharfe narrows to the Strid is to be in woodland glamour,
soft as a midsummer dream. The trees and the purl of ferny
streams are with you still as you climb towards the moor ; and
suddenly you reach a hollow where old, dead trees stand upright
with gaunt arms, or lie prone, their roots agape to the sky.
The Valley of Desolation it is named, and rightly. Once on a
day a storm broke here, of wind and lightning. It splintered
and scarred the forest oaks and elms. It struck deep into the
soil, so that the simplest, most confiding flowers are half-
fearful yet to show their faces.

Some say that a great crime was done here long ago—so dark
a crime that the skies themselves sent down the soldiery of
judgment. Others have it that a battle, dour and merciless,
was in the doing, that Heaven sent its legions to lay both sides
of the combat low. None knows. But the old, wiser sort of
farm-folk travel wide when they need to come home o' nights
past the Desolate Valley. It is a troubled hollow. The great,
happy woodlands circle it—part of the forest that knew once

the Cliffords' hunting-horn, the pad of outlaws' feet. Until our own day the wild deer roamed it, a herd sired in straight ancestry by the stags that gave many a gallop to the Clifford. Not long ago—yesterday, it seems—a herd old as Chillingham's wild cattle was with us in the Barden country. Forest fawns would surprise one as they moved willowy on the hill-crest, brown-grey among the amber mists ; and there were gloamings that showed a sudden pride of antlers, high on the moor-crest, traceried against the sky's dying crimson. It was in such moments that the centuries flung wide their gates and let one enter by right into Barden's storied heritage.

And now the deer have gone, they say ; but those acquainted with the forest's spaciousness, its lonely, deep ravines, know otherwise. So long as the woods give harbourage, there will be deer left to carry on the unbroken line from Clifford's day. One hale young buck at least escaped the slaughter, and a doe, for I encountered the pair not long since far up where the forest joins the moor. The buck challenged me roughly, glanced backward to see if his mate had stolen into cover ; then he, too, vanished as by magic. How could one help but reconstruct the romance of these two lovers ? When the havoc was ended, each had escaped the carnage by separate forest ways—had dropped at last from thirsty stress of flight—had slept in hidden lairs till the worst of their weariness was over, and then had crept to some neighbouring rill to slake their thirst.

For many days, I fancy, each wandered lonely—glancing constantly behind, remembering always the slaughter of their kindred, the terrible, salt taint of blood that drifted in the breeze's wake. Then suddenly they met in a clearing of the forest, and halted, wide-eyed with question. They recalled the lonely days, the nights when sleep had dread for bedfellow, the days of watchful terror. And now the loneliness was gone. There was only the luckless doe for him, and for her this lusty

forest outlaw. Of such marriages are born the strong children,
fit to re-people Barden's country of the deer.

One knows of other matings of this sort, of hidden glens that
hide each thrifty nursery ; and, when asked about the matter by
casual gossips, one meets intrusion by a devastating, cold lack-
knowledge. It is here, on the edge of the forest, that one knows
how futile it is to attempt extermination of the deer. Those left
inherited deep instincts. Their wits, keen enough at birth,
are sharpened by adversity. They will survive and breed
amain, and our sons may glimpse once more the dappled grace
of shapes that cross the forest roads like velvet shadows.

Another swift surprise is waiting at the forest-edge. A stride
takes you from shelter of the trees, and out into the naked moor
that climbs to Simon's Seat. The sky's borderland recedes.
About you is a sense of space and freedom, of great tenacity.
Whatever life persists here has earned its right of way, and
earned it by Homeric battle.

Simon's Seat—known as " Swart Simon " to his intimates—
stands, a sheer rock-fortress guarding these virile lands. On a
summer's day, long since gone by, one Simon, a shepherd, found
a man-child here. The babe was six months old or so, and lay
in a wicker basket, sheltered by the rocks from sun or storm.
The shepherd tugged at his beard awhile in great perplexity.
Unwedded, except to Dale, weather and sheep-tending, he was
appalled by this adventure. Then the bairn opened two blue
eyes at him, and kicked and crowed, reaching up his arms.
Simon knew what to do then. He took the child up, tucked
him away inside his coat, and sought a brother shepherd who had
a wife to understand such miracles as the " lile, snod thing that
cooed from under his coat." Soon afterwards the Barden
shepherds met in conclave. They put each a little from their
meagre earnings to the common fund, and reared the bairn
between them. And he was known as Simon Amang 'em,

because Simon the shepherd found him first, and because the others shared his maintenance. The Amanghams, a family scattered wide to-day, go to books and the Heralds' College for the meaning of their name. They should come instead to this rugged scarp of rock that gives its simple origin.

Whatever time of year one stands on Simon's Seat, there's winter's touch about the lands that climb to Greenhow Village.

Farmsteads, centuries old

Farmsteads, centuries old, dot the shallow valley below; but these are overmastered by pastures so far-sweeping, so shelterless and barren, that August's hottest sun can do no more for them than set splashes here and there of crimson heather, like fires too small to warm the body of a country starved and old. These are the wild lands, grim, silent, waiting for the true spring to come, waiting for a summer that at last will thaw their inner cold. Most of their streams run underground through great limestone river-ways and caverns. Sheep nibble everlastingly at wiry grasses, thin as the reedy, whistling breeze;

and hoody crows watch without ceasing for one of these to die of the lean herbage.

A land utterly desolate, you would say, till you get over to Greenhow, astride the hill-top, its weather-beaten houses planted anyhow along the track. Greenhow's people are astonishing in their self-reliance, their humour that can play or bite deep, their vigour for the forward tasks of life. They come of two well-blended stocks—farmers of the heights, and miners whose work was underground when lead was a rich ore to handle.

Greenhow, astride the hill-top

Wherever one wanders across these highlands, the mine-pits lie in wait ; and the story of each deserted shaft, if its mouldering props and beams could speak, would be an epic of hard strife, of courage that thought little of itself—and of ghostly happenings that were real as daily toil. It is useless for the inexperienced to mock at ghosts. Those who go down to the sea in ships habitually know that there are hauntings unguessed by landsmen. These old lead-miners knew, too, when they were accused of superstition by folk who stayed above-ground, the mystery things that happen in the underworld, where galleries probe into the tortured bowels of the earth, and the spirits prisoned there resent intrusion.

They were not fanciful men, the Greenhow miners, but quiet, stalwart, prone to say little. It was hard to break their reticence ; yet once in a long while they would speak of hidden matters. There was one who reached the mine-head before his fellows, and went down the ladders alone, impatient for his work. They came later on and found him dead in a narrow gallery, with queer marks about his throat. Well, poor lad, he should have known it was not good to go singly into any mine. The trolls fear numbers, but are wolves on the track of a lonely man. That was his comrades' summing up.

Then, too, there was the venture of a whole shift that went into the mine together and got to work as usual. At the end of an hour or so they heard the sound of footsteps down the ladders and along the gallery. They glanced at one another by the light of their candles and said that either they or the next shift were wrong about the time. Nearer and nearer sounded the heavy footfalls. Then suddenly they ceased ; and when the men went hurriedly to learn the meaning of it all, their lights flickered to and fro on emptiness. No other shift, mistaking the time, had come to relieve them. They understood the portent at last, and did not stay for words of any sort. With one accord they made for the ladders, reached the open safely, and again stood looking at each other, a little sheepishly.

The wind was so merry up here, the sun so heartsome, that they began to doubt their late experience of phantom footsteps. Pits were full of noises. Perhaps, after all, they had been like silly lads, letting fancies get the better of them. They were half inclined to return, indeed, when an uproar real enough sounded under their feet. They heard the ladders they had climbed by break and fall. Then one side of the shaft crashed inward bodily, and it was long before the echoes ceased to clamour upward to the open lands where the men saved by warning stood and doffed their caps with rough, instinctive reverence. Once again in the long story of the mines the Ghostly Shift had come to warn the living of disaster. And they say, as of a thing so assured as to be almost commonplace, that these Ghostly Companies were recruited from the ranks of miners who had died in shaft-falls. Their spirits lingered near the olden haunts, ready to go down into the depths again at need.

Men of Cornwall drifted to our northern highlands, following the lure of lead-mining. They brought with them the rich, Celtic gift of " listening to the other world," and their spirit-lore mingled with the ancient, native beliefs handed down by Norse and British ancestors of ours. To deal at length with the spirits that haunt the dim recesses of the mines on Greenhow would need a booklet in itself. Most of them were devilish—people of infinite malice and device, whose ceaseless labour was to oust the men who dared to probe into their underworld.

But not all were malevolent. Witness the Ghostly Shift, and the Knockers whose loud tapping is a sign trusted by all miners that they are nearing a rich seam. Witness, too, the testimony of a man who died recently among us. When he was in his teens he wandered over the Greenhow wastes in search of plovers' eggs, and the dark overtook him. Blundering this way and that, he stumbled over the brink of an unfenced mine, clutched at the timbers as he fell, and reached the bottom with no worse happening than a broken leg. Yet that meant death unless help came. And how should aid come, he lying at the bottom of a pitch-black shaft, and the fells overhead too dark for any wayfarer to cross ?

The goblins came about him—the wolf-pack that gloated on human prey—and they never ceased to pinch and bite him, and whisper in his ear that he'd best be done with life, lest they did worse to him than ever he dreamed of. He was of the breed, as it happened, that does not give in. One leg was useless, but he tried to clear a way with his fists—there in the wet, utter darkness—whenever the trolls assailed him. Then, at the worst of it all, when courage ebbed because life itself was dwindling fast, a light came down the mine-shaft, and following it a radiant figure that stood awhile and looked at him with a man's strength and a woman's pity.

A strange, desolate country, this of Greenhow

The maimed lad remembered how the Greenhow miners and the Cornish men had talked with bated breath of the Silver Spirit that was seen at times within the mines. His strength returned. Shout after lusty shout went up into the wastes; and a benighted shepherd, picking his way between the dangers of the land, heard the wild cries, and got to Greenhow, and brought helpers. Their lanterns went playing peep-a-boo with the dark across the silent pastures; and when, after hard labour, they got the lad to the mine-top, he tasted the bite of the night-wind greedily, and afterwards fell silent. It was a long while later that he told them he had seen the Silver Spirit of the mines.

A strange, desolate country, this of Greenhow, whose loneliness seems only deepened by the unsheltered road that winds

through it, a narrow ribbon of grey.   Strange and desolate, too,
is a fraternity which uses it day-long through all but the winter-
time.   Along the highway you meet or overtake slow-moving
figures, singly or less frequently in pairs.   Often you pass
a man asleep on the wayside grass, or sitting at a meal of broken
meat and bread that obviously has no meaning to his palate.
He eats because his body must be fed, and often ravenously.
For this is the Tramps' Road that connects two workhouses of
great strategic importance to the race : the Road of the Lost, if
ever there was one.   There is only one like it in the North, to my
knowledge—the highway over Shap Fell, set in the same grey
loneliness of bare, wide acres, peopled by wayfarers with the
same tramps' seal set on them for life.

To travel the Greenhow Road with a shrug of the shoulders
and the murmured catchword " wastrels " is as easy as to stay
at the top of a mine-shaft and disdain its hauntings.   To travel
it—often, and without prejudice—is to wade deep in surmise,
doubt, compassion.   One cannot help it.   These were once
red-blooded men, most of them, eager for toil and its rewards.
They wanted nobody's bounty, and the mere name of workhouse
was abhorrent.   When did the first step into the mire come
with each one of these castaways ?   And when the second, and
the long progression from shame to shame, till they reached the
stage where " *lost* " was written in every slouching step ?   For
each his own heart's bitterness, that drove him down and further
down.   For each this passive content, at the end of all, with
journeys from one workhouse to the next.   Yet it is no content.
Now and then you surprise a wild-beast, sombre fury in their
eyes.   They have remembered for a moment that they were
free men once.

And there are women, their faces quiet and sombre, who tread
the Road.   The same slouching gait is theirs, the same unbelievable dumbness to the joy of life.   Once, against my will,

I heard one of these tell her story, and was ashamed to be an eavesdropper. I was sitting at the open window of a Greenhow cottage. And first an old tramp came along the road and sat down on the bank across the way. Then he was joined by a woman, who dropped beside him from sheer fatigue.

" Tired ? " said the man.

" A bit more than tired," was all her answer.

By-and-by he asked slowly, and without seeming interest, what had brought her to the Road. And the years were broken up for her by that one question.

" Love of a lad," she said, her voice harsh with bitterness.

A life-tale crushed into a few bare words. And the Road of the Lost is strewn with such stories, if only the silent folk who carry them would speak. Mingling with the true, dour breed you meet once in a while a face with humour in it—jollity, even, if the day be sunny and the wind at rest. These are amateurs of the Road, as it were. They are down, but not yet " out " altogether, and hope is with them still. At the next corner, or the next, Eldorado will be lying in wait. Then they will wash themselves and feast, and make a jest of what has been. Boyish dreams survive ; and, till these are gone, they cannot let man-hood drift stagnant into nothingness.

What a brave, many-sided heart beats under Greenhow Hill's rough coat. He and his straggling village have faced life and weather in the raw for centuries out of mind. His kindliness is not apparent, except after long acquaintance. His flowers, too, are reticent, for they hide surprising beauties among crannies of the walls, or in the furrows of grim rocks, or thrive in bog-lands where men's feet seldom stray for fear of sinking. And what of Greenhow's outlook on the world below him ? The great ghylls stretch, sheltered and stream-fed, as far as his eyes can travel. Seen close at hand—not from far-off Simon's Seat— the crimson moors are big enough to warm the whole land at their fire. Nothing but mist can hinder Greenhow from seeing how it fares with Whernside, Buckden Pike, Penyghent and Ingleborough ; and, when he tires of Yorkshire mountains, he can glance aside with a hope of glimpsing Westmorland.

By standing fast in his own country, keeping watch and ward, Greenhow has learned secrets that he tells to few. Tales of wind and sleet and heat o' June—tales of the folk who passed his way, with blistered feet or light—are hidden in his rich granaries of memory. And out of his tireless love of the bleak homeland he has learned things bright and high as the stars, bright and

Lone Habitations

lowly as the glow of a cottage window, welcoming a man returned from usual toil.

Of modern folk who tread his highway, he loves best, I fancy, the navvies. There were more of them in the days when the big reservoirs were in the making down near Pateley; but some of a brotherhood always welcome still stray up the road in search of work. The navvy is so entirely of the Northern English, somehow. There is nothing vital that separates him from a clean-minded sportsman of any rank. A lady's honour is safe in his brawny hands. So is a man's life, if the man plays straight. He needs few things, but will have them, though riot and blood-shed be the price.

Freedom to work till the sweat drips from him, liberty after-wards for strong meats and ale, with a brawl and a cock-fight thrown in for recreation—these he must have. He fights fair, his appetite for the joy of life is Gargantuan, and he never forgets the least kindness shown him. If one of a gang working in the neighbourhood halts at your door on a raw windy night and borrows a match or two for the pipe that is " to take him up the hill "—whether or no you add the obvious courtesy of a stirrup-cup—you will find yourself sib to the whole company. The freedom of the camp is conferred on you. There is no ceremony, no fuss of any kind, nothing said ; but in twenty ways, big and little, you are made pleasantly aware of your distinction.

There is a wider fellowship to be attained—freedom of the Dale. It is seldom spoken of, and then only by another name. Yet it is real as the craggy land itself. So is its converse, though I doubt if ever at this day you hear the threat " to put the Dale on a man " ; but that, too, can be real enough in extreme cases. So little is asked of a candidate for this freemasonry, and yet so much. I have a suspicion that most of the credentials are summed up in the one word " jannock," to which delightful and staunch Yorkshire phrase there is no equivalent. Certain it is that, to this day, a freeman of the Dale can travel with empty pockets and a heart as light, if the fancy takes him, from Bolton up to Oughtershaw, and lack no meal or friendly greeting. For the other sort strange hindrances arrive from nowhere. Puck and all his imps seem loosed on them till, weary and befogged, they cry loudly for the meaning of it all. And no man replies.

Greenhow knows what goes to this freedom of the Dale. He has watched men earn it on the wind-swept, open highway, and in the valleys, and on the heights where shepherds labour ceaselessly, with rheumatic joints as their sure reward for toil. A wild land, clear-eyed and honest. A land whose beauty grows on one, year by year of knowledge. It is remote from huddled streets, and near the sky. Its soul is the free soul of the North.

VI

A LOST HAMLET

West End—A Forgotten Village—What Used to be.

TO stand on the roof of the world at Greenhow is to let one's fancy run out to other Yorkshire Dales. Deep out of sight below the rolling highlands yonder lie Nidderdale and PateleyBridge, its grey, comely capital, a market town with stories of its own that tempt a man to go down and linger with them. There's a beguiling road, too, that leaves the sanctuary of Greenhow's little hill-top church for a waste of heatherland and firs, a road that takes you to Blubberhouses, one of the oldest hamlets in the North. And, set in the middle of the rolling country between Greenhow and Blubberhouses, the patient searcher may stumble on another hamlet of arresting charm and deep significance.

First you come unexpectedly to an inn that seems to have been there always, so quietly it grows out of the landscape. An ancient signboard sways in the breeze. The tavern's front is small, and of no account; but at the back is a spacious yard, haunted still by fragrance of the days when post-horses were in demand and hoofs rang merrily along the roads of joy. There's honeysuckle all down the steep of the winding lane below the inn. Bees are drowsy. Somewhere a farmer calls his cattle to the milking. Green pastures climb to the sky. There is nothing to suggest that you will come, at the sudden turning of a corner, within sight of many dwellings.

This hamlet, when you reach it, has no human life that is obvious to the five senses. West End, they name it, and it lies in a deep pocket of the enchanted lands that roam down to the Washburn country. It was built when water-power was everything to the manufacturer, and distance from the towns of small account. The hamlet's walls are roofless now, but they give you the complete picture of what a mill-village was before

The Mill

steam set its grip on old-time England. The mill-master's house is there. What would now be a crude " dam," its waters unhonoured and unsung, is, in West End, a gracious mere. Wild duck breed among its sedges, and the goit that fed the water-wheel runs past what was once the mill-master's pleasant garden. He must have fished here, in his leisure hours, must have shot wild-fowl at the pool above. The very orchard trees, from which the fruit hung ruddy in his day, still blossom and bear, devotees of the world that understood once how to make commerce a comely and romantic matter. The ruins of the water-wheel are left, garlanded by ferns and kindly mosses. So are the well-built cottages of the workpeople, and the manager's house, and the lofty mill itself. It is all so thorough, this forgotten village. One feels, somehow, that they did not need to talk of democracy and betterment. They were true democrats, without need to realize as much.

They worked and played blithely in West End, a community self-sufficing and self-dependent. Its stones whisper that clear

None but spirit people live here nowadays

message to you. If you have patience, and the gift of listening rightly, there are other voices—laughter of mill lads and lasses released from well-paid work—prattle of children whose souls and bodies had liberty to grow. None but spirit-people live here nowadays. Not a single modern homestead has been built from stones so well-masoned and so abundantly at hand. It is as though the hollow had been guarded by hands invisible, so that it should give our generation a perfect history in little of what used to be.

The hideous days of child-labour in factories were over.

E

Men had scarcely begun to rear the manufacturing towns that now eat up, like a cancer, league after league of what once was God's country, jewelled with wildflowers and musical with tinkling streams. Commerce had dignity and ease; and the gracious humming of its looms, the droning of its water-wheels, were part of the wind's note on the upland—part of the spacious symphony of lark and throstle, plover and curlew, and wild-fowl winging free. As one gets up from West End, by the steep track above the gorge, a lump comes into one's throat, somehow. Just a lump comes into one's throat. No other phrase suffices.

The true democracy lived there. Merry England lived there, thrifty and work-proud, with clean laughter in her heart. And still, in the Lost Hamlet, the melody of gracious days remains.

VII

KNARESBOROUGH

Cromwell at Ripley Castle—St. Robert's Cave—Mother Shipton's Well —The Old Vicarage—Scriven.

HERE at Greenhow fancy returns from the Lost Hamlet only to beckon one away indefinitely into tale and legend clustering thick about old Nidderdale. Close at hand is the road that leads to Harrogate. They spelt it Harrowgate once, when belles and bucks of the Regency played the splendid fool there and had their little day. Ghosts of that bygone frippery and pompous ease roam still through the town's prosperous streets, as they haunt the Pantiles down yonder in the south at Tunbridge Wells. Story crowds on story, too, as one remembers doings that happened Dacre way, far down yonder in the valley—and at Ripley Castle, where Cromwell quartered himself for the night after Marston Moor, and Lady Ingilby, racked with terror lest her lord had died in that grim battle, held her visitor at bay.

Through the long night she sat vigilant on one side of the table, Cromwell on the other. And in her hand she held a pistol, primed and ready.

" Is this your hospitality ? " he asked.

" It would be my husband's sort, if he were here," said Lady Ingilby.

And so the long watch went on. A great painter has given us the scene, limned with reticence and eager strength.

Still further afield lies the country of the Scroopes. Some time when the Middle Ages were paradoxically in the first flush of youth, there was a fighting Archbishop of the race, who knew how to don armour of both kinds. Since then the race has survived, to carry on a tradition English to the core. Theirs is a romance built, not on costume and by-my-halidoms, but on the simple deeds of gentlemen who wore at heart the Yorkshire Rose.

Nidd, brown and tranquil, washes Knaresborough's feet

Here on Greenhow, astride the barren heights, Knaresborough, too, is apt to recur constantly to mind. The river-girdled town seems to grow clearer to the vision as memory roves from these grim highlands, in search of contrast, to the deep-hidden Dale of Nidd beyond.

Knaresborough, among the Dales' market-towns, has a place all its own. In situation and character it is like some pleasant foreigner come to settle in the North. Its colour is not made up of greys and lichen-greens—as Skipton's is, and Settle's, and many another town's. Its tiled roofs somehow give the place its subtle air of warmth and well-being. They have mellowed into shades of mulberry and brown and ochre that blend in unobtrusive harmony. Nidd, brown and tranquil, washes Knaresborough's feet. The blue-skied hill lands crown its head. And between the river and the heights is packed a wonderland of story. Like Skipton High Street, the town shoulders away the hurry and encroaching din of life; for it, too, is loyal to its memories. The cliff rises sheer from Nidd. Houses have been carved out of its solid rock, round about St. Robert's Cave—houses that go up, a room at a time, till the journey through them, beginning somewhere near the river, ends at the door opening to the fields above.

St. Robert's Cave alone holds in its little compass the story of all that was best in the Vision Splendid which lit the Middle Ages. St. Robert himself had been in many wars. A fighter to the marrow, he had known the heady tumult of blow for blow—known the salt sting of wounds, the lying-by times when women's eyes were kind and he strained at the leash of sickness, eager to be free again for battle. And suddenly a voice began to whisper at his ear; and he heard, but would not yield to it as yet. Peace was about the land once more—but who could know how soon there would be war again, and he be needed for the forefront of the strife? At heart, too, he loved battle as the breath of life.

The voice persisted, till at last its call was overmastering. Sir Robert put aside his knightly trappings, toiled painfully in the little cave high up the rocks till he had made a cell of it, just big enough to live in. He carved out, too, an altar-niche and a bed of stone on which to sleep; and as the years went on the fame of his quiet holiness spread abroad. The poor came to him for healing of their sores—whether body or spirit chanced to be afflicted—and he was tireless in their service.

To go alone to-day into that bare cell is to be caught up in a flame of understanding. No splendour of ritual, passed down the centuries, no pealing of organ-notes in dim cathedrals, can be as eloquent as St. Robert's Cave. The stone bed, the stone altar-niche, the silence broken only by the lap-lap of Nidd, are choired about by minstrels from behind the slender Veil. The candles that were lit on that small altar were brought by those scarce richer than himself. The poor brought, too, what little food he needed. And his great ministry went on, an inspiration and a song of praise, until one evening they found him on his bed, hands crossed above his breast, and about his face the Crusader's utter peace.

Knaresborough, indeed, is the home of realities that lie beneath the casual everyday. Across the river, within hail of Robert's Cave, there is Mother Shipton's Well, where she " practised divination, the old witch," as one of her detractors puts it. Divination was most certainly her gift, but she was in no sense a witch of the broom and brimstone sort. Knowing her gift, she followed its leading with selfless zeal. Broken in health, poor and derided, she never bent the knee to circumstance, or pawned her birthright by crossing palms with silver for promise of wedlock soon to come and other glib fooleries of the kind. She kept herself apart from traffic of the busy world, nursed the inspiration that was dear as a first-born child, and her memory stands to-day triumphant. What she said would come is here among us. Tennyson, when he sang of " aerial navies grappling in the blue," was her disciple without knowing it. Scarcely a foretelling of hers has gone astray. If St. Robert in his cave was a child of the New Testament, she was a child of the Old, a prophetess.

Men recall now, with a jest, that she foretold how a time would come to England when the seasons would not be known from each other except by the leafage or by the lengthening and shortening of the days. The seasons would be mixed together, with winter running through them all. To us in the Dales there's no jest in this fulfilment. In two recent years we had eight winters. The farmers watched lean stock nibbling starved pastures, saw their lambs die in spring and their meadow-grass come thin and brown to the hay-mows. They did not make a jest about it. The thing was real, the desolation close at hand.

This well of Mother Shipton's has a curious power that in older days suggested the miraculous. It is a " dropping well," and turns to stone whatever is suspended long enough amid its trickle. Sometimes, indeed, it wears the look of a gamekeeper's larder; for many furred and feathered bodies are brought to go through the slow stages of petrifaction.

Knaresborough's infinite changes are part of her beguilement. Every house built up the cliff tempts one to enter it with or without valid excuse. A gardener at heart builds his plot under any conditions that happen to surround him; and it is astonishing to see how rock-plants have been coaxed to thrive in pockets cunningly devised. Wallflowers, aubretia, arabis in white cascades—the saxifrages, red and cream and yellow—London Pride, all dainty in its pink and green—the cliffs are dressed as for a gala day. Yet go down to Nidd, and you find gardens of another sort entirely—soft, lush places, their feet in the water almost. The irises thrive here, and pæonies, and lavender walks. On summer evenings, when the dusk is warm and still, you ask for the nightingale and wonder that he dare not roam into our northern country.

One of these gardens has steps that go to the river and a mooring-place for skiff or punt. Few seem to remember nowadays that Charles the First once paced its borders in bitter tribulation. Knaresborough, like Skipton-in-Craven, had held out with gallantry; but the war in Yorkshire had gone disastrously for the King, and he was here, needs must, to sign the treaty of capitulation.

It was signed in the house attached to this old-world garden. The King sat on one side of the table, Cromwell on the other ; and that other picture starts to mind, of Lady Ingilby and Cromwell sharing a night's vigil at another table, bees-waxed so sedulously that the flickering candle-glow was mirrored in the oak. The house, at that time the Vicarage, was built in the days when " roof-tree " had a literal meaning. The great trunk, lopped of every branch, still carries the fabric of the house that was built round it in the olden way. Its haunting has been known so long as to be accepted as almost usual. I had the story from the tenant, a burly Yorkshireman, who would have been the last man in the world, you would have thought, to have traffic with the ghost-world.

" Of course the place was haunted. You couldn't live for a day in it without being sure of that. I never saw anything, but heard enough to last my lifetime—sobbings and cries, fit to break your heart while you listened. There were sharp, cold winds, too, up and down the passages, when the night was still as a churchyard. But I liked the old house, and stayed on."

People never unburden their hearts in this way unless they are sure their listener is reverent towards all ghost-lore ; and even then they are apt to fall into a shyness, curious and hard to win through.

" I didn't know who it was, gallivanting about the place," he went on, after a long silence—" till I'd a fancy to make a cupboard under the stair. And while we were making it, we came on a piteous thing. We broke through the boards and into the hollow under the stairway ; and there inside was a muddled heap of clothes—women's clothes. It was only when we lifted it up that the poor, naked bones shook out on to the floor."

His simple way of telling the story brought home its grimness

—brought, too, the wildest surmise and conjecture. A woman's mouldered raiment—a pitiful heap of bones—and silence absolute as to their history.

" The place *was* haunted, you said," I ventured by-and-by.

" It's ended now. Those bones were given Christian burial."

I can recall only one house with such strange mingling of interests as this old Vicarage, with its roof-tree, its haunting, its memories of King Charles and Cromwell. That other dwelling is the Mint House at Pevensey, in Sussex, where echoes of Norman William's day linger, and a tongueless woman moans and will not be quiet.

Wherever you wander, in and out of the town's ways and by-ways, some old tale is lying in wait. Even its modern market-day is like no other. The street is packed with booths. You can buy anything, from a ploughshare to a box of nails. In spring you find hand-carts laden with temptation. Double daisies, some red, some white, bring back remembrance of gardens known long ago, when the world cared for simpler flowers. And there are pansies, winking a shower away from their faces now the sun is out again. And herbs in plenty— thyme and rosemary, bergamot and tansy, rue and marjoram and lasses' love—all for your garden gay.

You can also buy—a merry, smooth-faced rogue assures you of it—a medicine whose prescription was given him during his travels in the highlands of Thibet. It will cure you of more ailments than existed, to your knowledge, until he names them; and its price is absurd, because he is a lover of his fellow-men. To smooth sickness from the furrowed brow is his delight. This elixir of health has been dearly bought by him, but he is not here for profit. That is why he is selling each bottle of the priceless mixture at a loss. This glib practitioner begins presently to single out individuals in the crowd about his rostrum, proves to each by skilled suggestion that he or she has a grievous malady, then bids them cease to worry any more. A bottle of his physic once cured the Grand Lama of Thibet, so surely lesser folk could trust its virtues. In amongst his serious business of convincing people that they are ill, he has a wide range of patter, a fund of anecdote that brings the ready laugh or the maudlin tear. One is absorbed by the man's genius, playing with a sure touch on the humanity he knows by heart.

It is an ancient mart, all its to-and-froings threaded by the mystery of unwritten laws. Its stall-owners, most of them, are ancestried by market-men who thwacked their ritual into the very bones of those to follow them. Over and over again a brand-new salesman has succeeded by purchase to a stall-right, and has taken his own way without heed of precedent. If he has been quick of apprehension, he has learned to fall humbly into line with centuries stronger than himself; if slow, or obstinate, they have a way of teaching him dislike of Knaresborough.

You cannot get away from antiquity. The Castle ruins are eloquent with strife of Cavalier and Puritan. When you have reached the high country bordering the town and got a little way into the fields and market-gardens, you come to Scriven village, a corner of the world left for man's delight, from the days when England was herself. There is order, without fussy neatness. The gardens fronting each good house are trim, yet free in their luxury of bloom. The tenantry of Scriven Park have their homes here, and all that was real and comely in times deceased elsewhere comes into quiet view. The old wives' tales of dark oppression, and poor folk trodden in the mire, are swept away. Here at Scriven are lusty survivors of an age that bred self-reliance and the happiest sort of pride.

Till lately there were Slingsbys at Scriven; and to speak of a Slingsby in the Dales, or in the country of the Yorkshire Wolds, is to sound a trumpet note. Clean-minded, clean-handed, strong for sport or battle, they built a glamour round the name—a thrifty glamour, strong to survive.

Standing here in Scriven's twilight, the mind roams up and down the Dale of Nidd. So many gallant families have gone from birth to burial, carrying the torch till younger hands were there to take it forward. So many yeomen, simple farmers and their hinds, have worked in peace or fought in strife, side by side with their overlords. Hampsthwaite and Dacre and tough old Pateley Brigg are thick with Dalesmen counted buried out of sight. Yet how surely they live on, so that you cannot miss the tramp of their lusty horses, their rollicking song as they go to hunt or market.

The April dusk gets to sleep with its dreams of elder days. From Knaresborough, old and wise, the market-folk come home. And the world goes very well.

VIII

PERCIVAL HALL

IT is hard to get away from Greenhow, tenacious of its own recollections, big with memories that linger round its steep descent to Pateley. Yet Greenhow knows, too, of old romances stored in many a corner of our Wharfedale side of the hill-crest; and the only trouble, as one turns for home, is to keep to the plain road. You cannot do it, somehow. A by-track shows on your left, leading into waste country that tempts and beckons. It brings you near again to Simon's Seat, where Skyreholme and its old paper-mill nestle in the valley. The wooden sluice that feeds the water-wheel drips pleasantly, high above one's head; and the wheel's thrifty, humming chant does not disturb the silence, but mingles with it.

High up the fells that look across at Simon's Seat, a grey house stands shelterless except for its few trees and the fields above its roof. Everything about it—its isolation, the sugges-tion in each rugged line that it was built not only as a homestead, but for defence—take one's steps that way. Seen close at hand, Percival Hall is simply a rich legacy, bequeathed us by an elder day. Unspoiled it stands, proud of its isolation and long mem-ories. At one end of the main dwelling is the " bride-house." Dower-houses are scattered in plenty throughout England—houses for the widowed mistress when the heir comes to his own

—but the bride-house is rare, and has a singular appeal. When the heir loved some lady who happened to find approval with his parents, they dowered him with the little house next door, and watched his bairns grow up. They had need to keep their men close in those days, need to pray for many men-children to be born.

A road corner

Not only the Scots came that way. The Percivals had feuds close at home—with overbearing neighbours, with gangs of lawless tribes that roamed the forests. They built this massive house of theirs for war, and so kept peace inside it at constant hazard. Every stone of this old hall is a guide to the Northmen's character to-day. They were not fathered by soft winds and gentle speech. Their reticence is neither cold nor harsh—it simply waits till it knows whether enemy or friend knocks at the outer gate. It has learned wisdom from forefathers whose teaching lives on, unguessed by the men who ply usual tasks to-day. But, once the stranger has won his way firmly through the gate, he finds a big, hospitable welcome that never varies as the years go by.

See Percival Hall in winter, with a nor'-easter piling up the snow-drifts. Its trees are bleak. Their branches groan and cry in travail. Simon's Seat thrusts a savage head into the turmoil. The farm-dogs yap and growl. Sturdy and grim, the Hall awaits whatever onset comes. Then go when summer is stepping tranquilly to autumn. The old house is at peace beneath its sheltering, full-leaved trees that show here and there a touch of the red-gold that will come with October and its pomp. Fruits are ripening in its garden. From far across the valley, Simon, mystical in trailing mists of blue and amber, looks over at a citadel that takes its ease. Truly the land, its houses and its people, are one in character.

In earlier days the Hall's succeeding occupiers were, by position, magistrates. There is a curious chamber, set apart once for housing such malefactors as had to be detained over-night. Small, but clean and dry, it stands above ground, and obviously has little kinship with the dungeons of more ruthless times. By a paradox delightful to all observers of life as it is—not as the copy-books would have it be—the only record of a tenant left to us is that Dick Turpin was "sheltered" here, when the police of those days were searching high and low for Richard.

He was "wanted" for a robbery somewhere on the York and Pateley road, and was not found. That is the tradition—a legend that opens out a whole country of controversy and surmise. Turpin was, in plain fact, an occasional frequenter of these northern heights ; but it is likely that Nevison, not he, was the highwayman sheltered by a magistrate at Percival Hall. In the same way, Turpin's supposed ride from London to York was borrowed from a real exploit of Nevison's. To cover some nine score miles in less than a day is, on the face of it, impossible. One man, with a relay of horses, might have done it in the reputed time ; but one horse could not, by any possibility, have carried a rider's weight so far and at such speed over the rough tracks of those times.

The ride to York, as history knows it, was made by Nevison, our northern highwayman ; and it started, not at London, but at Pontefract in Yorkshire. Nevison was a knight of the greensward after Robin Hood's own heart. Like Robin, too, he was of gentle birth ; for his father was York's premier physician, moving among people of all degrees with ease and a singular gift for the craft of healing. What took his son to the road, we do not know. Perhaps he wearied of the city's streets, the decorum asked of his father's profession. His blood may have been fired by much reading of the exploits of the outlawed Robin and his merry men. He chose his calling, however, once for all, and it meant a double life of a sort that must have tickled his abundant gift of humour.

His earliest exploit is typical of the man's whole outlook. Somewhere on a highway near York he encountered two farmers, standing in the roadway with woe-begone faces turned towards the west. He checked his horse to ask what ailed them. They pointed to three figures climbing the hill not far ahead, and explained that the footpads, armed with pistols, had held them up on their return from market and taken all they had.

" How much was it ? " asked Nevison.

When told that it was forty guineas, he bade them stay where they were till he rode back, and plucked his horse to the trot. Overtaking the three as they reached the hill-top, he demanded their surrender ; and, when one of them showed fight, he shot him through the pistol-arm. Afterwards, with great simplicity

and ease, he took all they had and sent them skulking for cover
lest worse befell them.

With the same simplicity he mounted again, rode back as he
had promised, and counted out forty guineas to the astonished
farmers ; for Nevison always had a fine contempt for what to
him were the outcasts of a profession whose gentlemen went
horsed, and he never preyed, moreover, on honest farmer-folk.

" Riding Will's " earliest exploit.

His fame by-and-by began to be noised abroad. "Riding Will,"
as he was known, grew in his own way to be the guardian of
lonely roads for the poorer sort of wayfarers. The cut-throat
breed of thieves, who jeered at under-sheriffs and their men, did
not laugh at Nevison. They laid plots for him instead, and all
of them miscarried. In York itself he became the toast of
dinner-tables. They did not know that Riding Will was the
Nevison who often dined with them and had to rise to drink his
own good health. Even the officers of law began to wonder

where they stood with regard to this rider who cleared their roads of footpad scum with more success than they.

One of these officers—jealous for promotion, doubtless—succeeded at last in capturing the elusive Will. As a matter of fact he caught him asleep in a tavern where, by all rules of the game, he should have been secure. The host, a lousy rascal taking pay from both sides, betrayed him; and Nevison was duly housed within the precincts of York Gaol. Then the rich comedy began. The Governor of the Gaol, a choleric, self-important fellow, bore Nevison a lively malice. It was not only that Will had robbed him in open daylight on a road eight miles out of York. To the ridicule of this was added the common knowledge that Nevison took toll from no gentry except rich niggards, or such as were credited with deserved unpopularity. Will, in fact, had become the test of a man's reputation; and the Governor, knowing it, chafed and fretted, until the good news came that his enemy was safely gaoled at last.

He visited the culprit in his cell, and gibed at him.

" How d'ye feel, Riding Will ? " he asked, his port-wine face glowing like a summer's day. " As jolly as when you robbed me on the Knaresborough Road ? "

Will knew the man, and the special fear that took half the pleasure from his well-paid life as Governor of the Gaol; and he played on that dread as on an instrument of strings.

" Not quite as jolly, sir," he muttered.

" Aye, that's the highwayman breed," mocked the Governor. " Brave enough till they see a rope in front of them."

" I've no fear of that."

" Then why are you trembling like a leaf ? "

" I couldn't tell you, except that it feels like gaol fever."

The Governor stepped back sharply. A pistol at his head was child's play, measured by fear of this pestilence that thrived in prisons. It was virulent. It passed from man to man with the speed of a moorland fire, and few survived.

" There are no spots yet that I can find," said Riding Will ; " but there's a sickness in my body."

" I'll send the prison doctor," snapped the Governor, in hot retreat.

An hour later the doctor came. He was a good sort, and therefore sworn friend to Nevison. The turnkey who let him in retreated in passably good order, for whisper of gaol fever had already got about the prison ; and then the two men talked together.

" Oh, be quiet, fool Will," snapped the doctor presently. " Men with fever don't laugh like that. They may hear you."

" They'll be sure I'm in delirium," said Will, with another roar of laughter. " And what d'ye think of my plan, Doran ? "

" It carries," chuckled the other ; " and lucky it is that I'm still a dabbler with paint and brushes."

Doran then sought out the Governor, expressed his opinion that Nevison was in the throes of fever, and left with the assurance that he could give a clear decision on the morrow. The next day found him closeted again with the prisoner, and after awhile he stood back to admire his handiwork.

" The finest picture ever painted, Will," he murmured glee-fully. " Beautiful, authentic plague-spots, all of 'em. They might call in every practitioner in York, and they'd agree the symptoms are plainly there."

" How do I look ? " asked Nevison, with boyish curiosity.

" How ? Why, you'd run away from yourself in terror, man, if I had a mirror to hold up."

Doran, his task with the brush accomplished, went to the Governor once more with the grave news that Nevison un-doubtedly had the fever.

" You had better come and see him, sir," finished the doctor briskly. " You'll find it a singularly bad case."

" No, no," snapped the other, edging away as he had done yesterday from Nevison's cell. " That's your province, Doran. Keep me informed of the man's condition."

Doran kept him informed. That afternoon the highwayman was worse, and by evening he was officially dead. With extreme haste the Governor ordered a coffin to be brought to the prison and the body interred in the place outside the city reserved for such as died in pestilence.

The undertakers came, and in their haste forgot to screw down the coffin-lid. No onlookers lingered near the dreary spot where a grave lay ready. So none watched Nevison come out of his coffin and grip the hands of boon-comrades who had been his burial men. He helped to shovel the soil over what should have been his own husk, thanked them afresh, and felt a sudden vertigo. After all, he *might* be lying there. His quick fancy got the better of him. Sweat drenched him from head to foot. Loth to show his weakness, he crept away to the road's silence, its free breezy air ; and there, at home with old adventures, the song came into his heart again.

The Governor, as it chanced, in extreme fear lest he took the fever, had decided at last that a ride abroad would clear his brain of whimsies. He came into the open country. The moon, bright and eager with the land, showed him a big, lean fellow coming to meet him on the road. He drew rein with instinctive dread, and the wayfarer came to his stirrup.

" It's Will Nevison," stuttered the affrighted Governor.

" All that's left of poor Will. He's come back to the roads he loved."

" But, damn it, man, ghosts don't carry plague-spots ! "

" I forgot to take them off," said Will, with a sepulchral laugh, and drifted ghost-like up the road.

The true tale of that night's doings was not known for a long while, except to a favoured company of intimates. But the superstitious side of the affair served Nevison well. A man dead and buried of the plague was obviously a ghost, if he held up travellers on the road. The whispered name Nevison was better than a pistol in his hand; and so he throve, and made

Percival Hall and the Bride-House

merry, and drank his own health again at York's exclusive tables.

There is no doubt that Dick Turpin did wander now and then as far from his London haunts as the Greenhow country, and legend supports history. Near the road between Greenhow and Harrogate, an old map shows a wayside barn with the name "Turpin's Lair," and country stories gather thick about his exploits in "the long-since days." Incidentally, this Turpin's lair brings a sheer joy in Dale words, occurring where one least expects them. The name suggests, on the surface, that a hunted man went there for refuge ; yet lair has always held a deeper meaning for the Dalesmen. It is a name, like that other fragrant title " mistal," for a place where cattle take their rest o' nights. Dick Turpin was wont to shelter in the cow-byre, and endowed it with his name.

It was from this same grey, four-square building, maybe, that Turpin emerged for the gay adventure remembered yet in story. He went a-robbing one moonlit night, and heard the tippety-tap of hoofs along the road. The tinkling sound came nearer. He pictured a traveller, plump of body and of purse, and trotted out to meet him. They met round a sharp bend of the track, the wayfarer and he. Both had pistols out, and both wore masks.

" Oh, damme, dog does not eat dog ! " laughed one of them.

" But, Will Nevison, it's your voice meets me. I'd rather hear that than the squeal of a fat merchant riding home."

" There's a convenient tavern near us, Dick. Suppose we put our pistols up, and sup together ? "

A legend in cameo, such as one finds often in this lone countryside. Old tales and ancient memories are instinct in the air that breathes about the Hall. New days come and go, and leave its chimneys sending up their tranquil smoke in greeting to Simon's Seat, across the wide valley. The little, grey bride-house suggests romance as eager as west winds in the spring. And not far away is a gorge that narrows to what is known to this day as Nevison's Leap. His horse took it at a stride, they say, what time they hunted him with a squad of riders far-flung from York. Undoubtedly Will Nevison, devil-may-care, instinct with chivalry and jest, gives Percival Hall its soul.

IX

ELVES, STRAY HAUNTINGS AND VILLAGE SCHOOLS

Primitive Phantoms—A Haunted Stable—The Ghostly Hound—The Brown Man of the Moors—A Troubled Spectre—Churn-Milk Peg— Pam the Fiddler—Holy Wells—The Soul of a Garden.

THE Dales are old enough to be sure of matters hidden from the hurrying world outside. From ancient times the fairies have been with them, the brown men who lurk among the heather spaces, the trolls that haunt deep ravines where the streams go on silent feet, afraid lest any noise of theirs should rouse the spirits. Goblins are busy in the old mineworkings on the moors. The Strid, near Bolton Priory, has its White Horse that comes from the racing flood, a warning of disaster to him who sees it. These are age-old, primitive phantoms ; but ghosts of the human sort, belonging to later days, are with us, stirring softly through our tales.

A strange haunting is attached to a stable of Percival Hall itself. The tale is persistent, told with downright, staid simplicity by many honest folk. One cannot let such evidence go by, as of no account. No horse is ever happy in this stable. If brought there in midday warmth, it shivers as it enters, and kicks and fidgets, refusing food. If left to all the dark can do, it is found next morning creamed with foam of terror, and turns haunted eyes on the master when he comes. Some stark tragedy has happened within the stable's walls. None can tell you how it went, though always there's a hint that Black Bess was stabled here often, and that somehow her ghost came to this ancient haunt after she died in carrying Dick Turpin from London to York. A likelier explanation, one thinks, is that Nevison's favourite horse—the steed that galloped under him from Pontefract to York, in time to prove an *alibi*—was quartered here at Percival Hall so often that, after his master's death, he roamed out by well-known tracks to let his heart break in the familiar stable. Men seldom find grace to die of heartbreak when the loved one goes ; but dogs and horses have that sort of constancy.

They have, too, a sixth sense given them, sensitive and keen. There's a barn on one of our high pastures that lies derelict to-day. Strong and trim-built, it had generations of usefulness before it ; but its owner let it go at last, because no dog would approach it unless dragged there by sheer force. A murderer lodged once among the hay in this same barn, till the hue-and-cry of an outraged countryside found him in his lair and haled him to the gallows. His tarred body creaked for many a day afterwards at a near-by cross-roads. Unshriven, lonely, restless, his spirit still lingers round the spot. At least, all dogs are sure of it ; and sceptics find it hard to invent reasons, other than the obvious one, for this terror of the thing unseen by men.

Dogs have their own ghosts, too, among us. There's a lane that goes from Cracoe, past the hollows that once were fish-ponds of the Nortons, and on to Rylstone Church. It is known right into our own day as a haunt of Barguest, the pad-footed hound. And there are other lanes—up the moors, and in savage ghylls among the waste lands, or down in the neighbourhood of wimpling streams—where folk go afraid, because of the ghostly cold that brushes past them, and the shaggy hound that journeys on before.

It is easy to dismiss such matters with a reminder that we live in modern times. We do ; and not long ago I talked with a usual man, healthy of mind and body, good at all field-sports, who let his under-mind speak out. It was commonplace knowledge to his family that they had a guardian hound, not of this world. Whenever disaster threatened, a great, yellow dog would meet the doomed one on the road, or by the coppice. It would go on before, glancing backward constantly. At the house-door it would vanish; but through the night a low, incessant howl would wander through the outside murk. All in the house had heard Barguest, not long before I heard the story; and the next day they brought his father from the hunting field, a dying man.

These realities are not to be explained, or laughed away. The true line of division between north and south goes, not by way of Tweed, but by the border limits of our Yorkshire highlands, and you will find our Dales' ghost-lore linked closely with the Scots'. The House of Airlie, far away in Scotland, knows well the summons of its Ghostly Drummer. At Glamis they understand the tragic stir of many hauntings. The Pass of Glencoe will not be still, because of what happened where the hills recall a foul and ancient treachery. Culloden Moor can find no sleep o' nights. For ever it remembers. And many a northern glen is restless, where the mists steal over, thick with ancient sorrows, and old, stark feuds leap from the unforgetting past. What else should be, but ghosts of many sorts in a country of grim highlands and rough story? What else could happen, too, except a sure faith in fairies, dancing flower-like through the roughness of our lives?

Elboton, guarding Thorpe-in-the-Hollow, is a special haunt of Wharfedale elves, as we shall learn. So is Waterford Ghyll, dividing once the Norton and the Clifford lands. They are seen to-day in the little wood near Threshfield school—not half a mile away as I write—and in a place of rocks up-dale where the water bubbles out from Robin Hood's Cave—and here and there among bosky hollows that nestle under the scarp of savage cliffs.

It is easier by far to disbelieve in fairies than to see one. I have met folk in plenty—credible folk—who have been in touch with phantoms of one sort or another. But one seldom finds an authentic witness to the truth that the Little People still live on. High-spirited, mettlesome folk, they, if lore of the countryside is to be accepted. Wayward in temper, but sound at the core of their tiny hearts, they only ask rough men to treat them with decorum and nice courtesy. The more one dips into their long

A special haunt of Wharfedale elves

history, indeed, the surer one grows that they have always been apostles of neighbourly good humour. If Robin Goodfellow clouts you on the ear, or makes you fancy that your body is thick with thistle burrs, take it that the displeasure is well earned, and set about to heal it. If ladies of the tribe pluck their slender skirts away as you approach, there's something wrong about you. Old people, who lived in the days of simple vision, tell you lore of this sort.

They tell also of Redcap, a great, little man at all kinds of indoor work—washing of crockery and what not—for as long as you humour his dignity. But he's quick to take fire at the least affront. They speak of Kilmoulis, too—a squat, lazy man-toad that basked by corn-millers' hearths and brought luck if he was left undisturbed. They have glimpsed the Brown Man of the Moors in their time. Riding home across the heather, they have seen this dwarf, big-headed, wide of shoulders, with a shock of tousled hair and clothes russet as October's brackens. He lies in wait for every traveller, challenging him to combat; but the prudent wayfarer jogs forward, stilling his horse's fright as best he may.

There's not a moor-road, or a field path, but is beset by its own haunting. Men and women have travelled these ways since the Dales were young—travelled them through centuries that would be forgotten if a ghost did not rise at the right hand or the left to remind one of things unforgettable. What of a certain field-stile near Appletreewick village? For many years a spectral figure would appear there at intervals, till at last a man came by who had courage to halt and ask what he needed. The reply was instant; for this lone, exiled spirit had been waiting, as such do, for a passer-by with wit to understand his trouble.

The story he told was so simple as to be matter-of-fact. In his life-time he had been prompted by greed to remove his neighbour's landmarks. High up the pastures was a field divided by a few rough " stoups " of limestone to mark the dual ownership. Little by little, working in the grey times of dusk, he had shifted first one, then another, of these stoups, till he had stolen a wide strip of ground. His brother-farmer, happy-go-lucky and unobservant, had suspected nothing. None had seen the theft. But from that day the spoiler's luck was out. Bad went to worse. Then came outright ruin, and after that a headlong rush into the abyss that waits for suicides. That was the tale. Asked again what he needed, the filmy lingerer on this side of things craved that the stoups should be restored to their right places, and added a plea that in its littleness was strangely full of pathos. The poison he had taken as an end to this life had been got from a chemist in Skipton, and the debt was still unpaid.

From start to finish the tale goes its simple way, not touched anywhere by lights of obvious romance. They traversed the far pasture, and found tokens that the stoups had been removed. They went to the Skipton chemist, whose memory happened to be fresh about a slender purchase made a few months before. They paid the poison-debt, restored the landmarks to their ancient stations; and the countryside was freed from an unhappy visitant.

If persistent unfaith in ghosts suggests to minds of a certain type that such tales can satisfy only rustic wits, I would suggest in all good humour that Dales wits are keen as the weather that has fathered them—alert and ready, with parry and thrust that reminds one constantly of rapier-play. No idle story has any but the shortest life among them; and such traditions as this queer haunting of the stile are always rooted deep in actual happenings.

Not all these earth-bound people, it would seem, are here in expiation of their sins. Some choose to stay from sheer goodwill to toilers who have not passed beyond the Veil as yet. How else can even cold logic explain the Little Light on a moor far up the dale of Wharfe?

It is a bleak and treacherous moor, with peat-bogs bordering green marshes and sullen bogs. A hard country to pick one's way through in full sunlight; but, when the mists come down, impassable. In such hours of need travellers have been known to glimpse a small, slow-moving light that goes ahead—as link-boys used to carry torches through city fogs—and the figure carrying it, dark in outline, is filmy as the night itself. If followed in quiet trust, this lantern of the mists guides the feet as by magic between the marshes and the bogs—the bogs that draw down their victims inch by inch into a peaty slime, chill as death itself.

A friendly sort of apparition—kin somehow to Robin Goodfellow—is Churn-Milk Peg, an ancient dame whose special work in life is to scare youngsters caught in the act of plucking nuts before they're ripe. Churn-Milk is our Dales name for the kernel of a nut before it ripens, and Peg waged ceaseless war against the spoilers. Sometimes I fancy she should be canonized, a patron saint, not of hazel trees alone, but of other comely growths, such as faith, romance, the lore of old, unhurried times. There are so many up-grown children nowadays who are all for plucking fruits before they're ripe; and the Dead Sea taste must be appalling.

The Dales know another ministry, invisible, that haunts it with eager, soft persistence. Its Holy Wells are abundant. At Burnsall—and near Friar's Head, on the way from Winterburn to Gargrave, where the Scots burned nine churches once— and in many a corner of the uplands you find these brimming well-springs. There is one at the garden-foot of the Pilgrims' Rest House, this side of Girston Brigg. The house draws its water to-day from the spring that lies scarcely higher than the river's margin, and to those who live there it is everyday knowledge that, however Wharfe may rise and lash her creaming banks, the Lady-Well prevails. The same storms that bring the river down in spumy passion feed, too, the well's deep, upland channels. She holds her own, keeping Wharfe at bay; and clear water comes always to the tilted bucket.

Two generations since, or thereabouts, a Girston tinker, coming by way of the Threshfield school on a nipping winter's night, was assaulted by the ghost of Pam the Fiddler. So legend tells the story. The tinker ran for dear life, and took refuge in Our Lady's Well. Pam snarled round him, knowing he was impotent to put his spell on a man standing firm in holy water, but finding consolation in his certainty that the tinker would take his death from exposure before the long, bitter night was ended. Till dawn and the first cock-crow, Pam kept his grisly watch and ward ; and after he had fled, perforce, the tinker got to solid ground again. He expected stiff joints, as Pam had threatened, but instead his limbs were light to carry him, and from that sojourning in ice-cold water he took a forward lease of life.

Under this tale, told racily and with self-excusing humour by the native-born, there lies a deep and ancient faith in the power of certain wells. Dread of ridicule holds men's tongues, but the belief is rooted more firmly than they understand.

If you will give one of these Holy Wells leave to speak for itself, go to that silent corner of the world beyond Friar's Head— itself a marvellous reminder of the times when men had heart and leisure to build dignity, charm, almost the spoken word, into a grey house-front. The roadway is scarcely aware of modern traffic. Its present days are threaded by memories of hoof-beats, of farmers jogging home from market, of hunting folk who returned on many a bygone dusk, tired and happy, astride weary horseflesh. It lives with what some name dreams, and others dear realities.

Helen's Well lies at a bend of this road, its sanctuary guarded by a low, mossy wall. Neglected for years out of mind, it retains still clear traces of what it was in older times. An unfailing spring comes softly up among stones carved with heart-whole joy in chiselling. Scattered now, these stones were once in orderly array about what is not a well, in the usual sense, but rather a wide rock-pool, deep here and shallow there, with little trees that murmur in the breeze above. Give yourself to this place, frankly and with the simplicity it asks. It does not preach, or scold, or rustle with the threat of unguessed ambushes among the grassy margin. Out of its inmost heart it gives you all it knows of life. The pilgrims coming with their sores, of body and soul, were not reticent. The Well heard tales that were foul with infamies of the world beyond its sanctuary. Men came with blood-guilt on their hands, and in their souls a blackness and a terror. Women knelt here in bleak extremity of shame. The Well heard all, and from its own unsullied depths sent up the waters of great healing. And the little chant of victory began to stir about the pilgrims' hearts, like the first south wind in April that breaks the winter up. And afterwards the chant gained in volume. It seemed to them that they were marching side by side with countless, lusty warriors who aforetime had battled for their foothold up the hills. And, after that, a peace unbelievable, and the quiet music of Helen's Well, as her waters ran to bless the farmward lands below. All this is there for you to understand to-day, if you will let the Well explain the richness of her heritage, the abiding mystery of her power to solace and to heal.

The Dales, packed as they are with hauntings of many kinds, yielded me once the strangest ghost-lore a man could well encounter. It lingers still in memory, that casual meeting, and recurs when life seems warped and tired.

The old, grey-haired woman was sitting in a wayside field as I came through. She had a basket at her side, and her blue eyes were looking into dreamland—brave, clear eyes, young with hope. Aware of intrusion, she came reluctantly from another world, and passed the time of day.

" I was gathering posies," said she, with a smile of self-excuse, " posies for remembrance."

The voice was low and strangely pleasant. A closer glance showed that every line of her tattered raiment fitted her slenderness as if she had been gowned, not by adversity, but by a skilled and cunning artist. The field—no more than a little croft, bordered on one side by a ruined barn—was bare of all but grass and nettles. What posies could be gathered here ? She caught the question, and pointed right and left with a gesture of quiet, happy confidence.

"Cannot you see them—gillifers and pansies? And clove pinks are winking the dew from their eyes in the border yonder."

I saw nothing but the untidy croft—that, and the beauty of her eager face.

"You cannot catch their scent?" she went on, with a troubled pity for my shortcomings. "There's all the flood of summer here—bergamot and tansy, lavender and rue—and lasses' love, the best herb of them all."

Once there'd been a garden-space

I chanced to have lasses' love in my own garden—a beguiling plant, lavender-grey and bushy, sending a cloud of golden blossom up when August lights the heather-moors above with crimson flame. So from that we got into fellowship, and she let her heart find room.

"You're young, as I count years," she said, with a smile that gathered up the grief and joy of things. "You go building your garden still. You've strength to do it. My own gardens, since life left me poor, are all of yesterday."

I shall never know her story. If it were given into my hand, a printed screed—a human document, as the slang of our modern day has it—I should not glance at it. Enough for memory is the still contentment of her face as she told me—there in the empty, barren field—how she had one little gift vouchsafed her—that of knowing always where once there'd been a garden-space.

"And in this garden," she said gently, "they planted musk about the border-stones. *It has not lost its scent.*"

So she, too, understood the perplexity of all gardeners to-day. From Cornwall to our northland heights—from Sussex to the Scottish border—men are searching for one single plant of musk that gives out the old, pleasant savour ; and they cannot find it. But this wayside devotee of gardens had recaptured the truant fragrance. She told me then how no after-neglect could kill the soul of a garden rightly planted and tended faithfully ; and something stirred, down in a deep-hidden corner of my heart. Any man who has tended his garden through lean years, digging hard, and planting thriftily, sparing no toil in rain or shine, knows the little, nagging question that comes time and time. What if one has to leave it all ? It seems unbelievable that one should be asked to till no more the borders that have learned to listen for one's footstep. No stranger could ever know their intimate, dear needs. The newcomer might do his best, but would not the garden pine and sicken for the intimate, quiet sympathy which the years have made secure ?

At such hours an odd question comes unbidden. If one had to go out into the wilderness, what plants would one take from the garden-space ? There would be pæonies, of course, and clove pinks, and many saxifrages. Nor could you leave behind the plant known to botanists as the Cashmere Primrose, but to us as Dear Harbinger, because she flowers bravely at the snowdrop time and does not wait for spring's gentler airs. Harbinger is a miracle to those who see her beauty for the first time, and her wonder never stales with long acquaintance. And how could you leave the aubretias behind, the sea-thrift, the daffodils and wood-hyacinths that people the spinney by the stream? Your selection grows apace, till you would need a roomy carrier's cart to share your journey to the wilderness.

Then you thrust nightmare doubts behind. The garden is still yours, asking only to be tended. Barrow and fork and spade are close at hand, tired of inaction while you dream of what may never happen in your lifetime. You must leave it one day, of course, when the drums call you up over the last Hill of Beyond. Soon or late, your garden is bound to be widowed and forlorn. But my wayside comrade, with the eyes that are seeing forward, explains, in a mystery of silence, that folk will come by way of one's old garden, and know it truly planted. Smell of the musk, perchance, may linger there—fragrance of gillifers and pansies—and overhead, I pray, a litany of rooks, settling into cumbrous sleep among the sycamores. After that, the hunting cry of owls, and a little wind against the casement— and then, far down the road, the "loppety-lop" of a farmer's nag as he rides from market barter to the freedom of a windy Dale.

Such hopes lie deep in the natural heart of the older country-folk. Will they survive among the youngsters of the Dale? They will, as long as our village schools are left to their own ordering. Wharfedale's schools have an atmosphere peculiarly their own, and the mere thought of elves and fairies brings Barden's little school-house clearly to one's mind. It stands at what is perhaps the most beautiful highway-corner in all England. Backed by a friendly belt of woodland, rising to the moors, it fronts grey Barden Tower. Below tower and school, the road winds down to the bridge hoar with legend, takes Wharfe in its long stride, and climbs to the pine forest and the moors beyond. Forest and heath and river are part of the children's lives as they go to school and home again. They are taught what other children learn; but through their tasks the magic of a country-side, rich in old-time lore, spins threads of true romance. Their mistress is an aider and abettor, one suspects; she for has the gift of seeing fairies in the hollows, goblins on the moor, of hearing the Cliffords' hunting-horn still busy on the hills, as if the brave mediæval times were not yet deceased. That is why her scholars are apt to go far in life.

Another little school stands at the foot of the raking bend that goes from Skyreholme to the Pateley Road. Again it is surrounded by free, open lands, by breath of the heather and the undersongs of old tradition. Percival Hall is near, and Troller's Ghyll, and friendly Simon's Seat across the valley. It, too, puts the soul of things into the adventure of arithmetic and spelling.

A Wharfedale school

So does Burnsall's Elizabethan School, fronting to-day's hurrying road with dignity and quiet. Above is the church, older by far than Elizabeth's day. And over kirk and school the high moors sweep to the open pastures and the climbing firs.

Linton's school, in the hollow near Lile Emily's crooked bridge, has the same sort of beguilement, threading routine of work with the warmth of old romance; and here, as at Barden, the mistresses know how to till the rich garden of a child's heart. The coppice just beyond has been known for centuries as a stronghold of the elves. Seeing's believing, as one small child averred not long since, with quiet and unassailable conviction. It seems indeed to be a truism that there are more fairies in the world than people who can see them.

THE FAVOURED VALE

UNDER the waste lands leading from Greenhow to
Wharfe River there lies a hollow of astounding, swift
romance. Appletreewick village runs all down its steep
hill into this hollow, and it seems old as the hills themselves,
grey, self-contained, austere in its picturesqueness ; only its
name suggests the drowsy hum of bees in orchard blossoms.

The Hall that stands at its top is massive, full of the dignity
that is part, too, of the thick-thewed elms that keep watch about
it. Its outbuildings are spacious ; the herbs in its garden are
scions of a stock that throve in the days when housewives knew
the virtues of all the simples and were not too indolent to brew
healing physics. The very grindstone in the corner by the far
laith brings that charm of eld which is beyond explaining.
Within there is a Minstrel Gallery, with oaken beams that were
once a forest tree, grown from an acorn, wind-sown in the dim
ages on some neighbouring slope. It is sufficing, this Hall
of ancient lineage; and sufficing, too, is the story of one
who came to its ownership and carried the honour with abiding
gallantry.

William Craven's tale, if one omits the cat, is precisely Dick
Whittington's. Born of Appletreewick stock, he spent his early
years in the Dale, was fired by ambition to dig gold up from

London's streets, and went thither on a carrier's cart that took three weeks for the journey. He found lowly service with a merchant of the city, worked his way up the ladder of advancement, and married his master's daughter. When the seventeenth century was very young—not quite in its teens as yet—he became Lord Mayor of London, and was knighted.

There is nothing singular in all this. No city could live for three generations unless its arteries were infused with red blood from the country. What is arresting in Sir William's romance is the inner lamp he kept alight throughout the days of his prosperity. His pride harked ever back to the country that had bred him. Before he left his Dale he had won the knighthood of a deep and selfless caring for the land that had bred him, for the folk who were his people. Over and over again, in those thrifty days of exile, he must have yearned to stand just where one is standing now—on the roadway bordering Appletreewick Hall, with Simon's Seat rugged and wise above the pine-woods and the moor. He would remember how, between the storms of March, great floods of sunlight chased the grim cloud-wrack out of sight—and how, in the year's riper days, a glory and a flame were flung wide from breaking heather-bloom. He returned to his birthplace, and bought the Hall that had fed his dreams in days gone by. Riches brought no arrogance. Plenty, and doffing of caps when he took the village street, only quickened his simple gratitude to life. He was a knight indeed, for the common rumour of his day has no casual gibe at his claim to be without fear and without reproach. He built Burnsall Bridge, for men lusty as himself to cross—over to Appletreewick, where he was born.

The next link in his family chain was another William Craven. A soldier to the bones of him, he went abroad to fight for the King of Bohemia, struggling against harsh odds. And there he found the King's Consort, sister to our own Charles the First—

found, too, a company of English gentlemen whose every thought was clean-hearted to guard the hapless Winter Queen. Through troubles unbelievable, through panic and rough journeys, William Craven was the leader of her gentry. He brought her safely over to England when the last hazard came ; and afterwards they stood in the fireglow together one wintry evening, and she thanked him for his services.

"What reward, my Knight ? " she asked. "Nothing is too much to claim."

"Yes, one thing is," he said—and said no more till her two hands were on his shoulders.

"You are so proud—proud of your humility. Have we not lived in camps together, you and I ? "

A wonder and a joy were showing now in Craven's face ; but he told himself this thing could not be true. He had worshipped from afar so long. This widowed Queen must always be remote from such as he.

"Ah, dull and stubborn ! " she said, with quiet raillery. "If I were a beggarmaid and you the King, show me how you'd play the part."

"If I were King," said he, with rough eagerness, "I'd build you golden steps right up to my throne. I'd take your hands in sight of all the people, and tell them you were mine. And I'd laugh with joy to know it true."

"If I were Queen—who am one no longer, save in name— I'd marry where my heart was. And it's yours."

So Craven knew it true, and kissed her, not as royalty, but as a woman ; and from that betrothal came a marriage, secret and guarded jealously, but happy as a song of old romance. Proved by harsh and slippery ways, they came into their kingdom. There were no threads about it, such as jealous Eleanor traced, to find her King and Fair Rosamond together. There was just their fine and equal needing of each other, the sufficing glamour that lived with them like sunlight and free air. When Charles the Second came to his own at last, William Craven the Second had a well-earned earldom given him. It was not bought with money, or earned along the roads of politics. It was given him for single-hearted devotion to a cause that had gone through evil times, with scant reward to offer until now.

Nowhere in all the Dale, perhaps, will you understand so completely as here at the High Hall the meaning of England and her strength. Such stalwart hamlets, hidden seemingly in a far backwater of the land, are part of national history. They have sent their sons, reared on upland weather, to take their full share in the world's affairs. The best of these have come north again constantly for communion with their own hills and folk, and so the life of town and country has intermixed. And one realizes all afresh how true is that old saying, "The country could live for ever without the towns, but not towns without the country."

As one leaves the High Hall and goes down the road, the sense of hoar antiquity is paramount. Fountains Abbey has left its imprint, here as in most Dales villages, and the house known as Monk's Hall is astir with whispers of half-forgotten things. Right at the foot of the steep village stands the Low Hall ; and this is as spacious—house and clustered outbuildings mossed over by the gentle gardener, Time—as its neighbour on the hill. It also housed a family—the Sedgwicks—that is known to-day with honour wherever Dalesmen gather.

It had a great fair once, this proud and trim-kept village. Scottish ponies from the wilds of Galloway and black-faced sheep made up the chief traffic. The raiders of the time before Flodden had become now a pastoral folk, making more by barter than ever they had claimed by pike and broadsword. Onions, too—known as "winter beef"—were in brisk demand. To this day the pleasant track branching down to the farmstead at its foot is known as Onion Lane, reminder of the times when it was set thick with stalls that sold this good commodity. Three days the fair lasted, and every corner of the street had its booth to tempt money out of purses. Trinkets and onions, broadcloth and linen, and charms to scare away the witches—all were mingled in wild disarray. The gypsies, too, gathered in force— Faas and Smiths, of a lineage outlasting centuries of change— the Tinkers ever at feud with them—the Merry-Andrews, who played six instruments at once, with mouth and head, feet and nimble hands — the beggars asking alms, and bonnie lasses who had slept over-night in some sheltered cottage and had wakened to the hum of bees among the lavender beneath their open dormer-windows. Lean shepherds from the hills were there, and surely, if they were not carting doliums of wine from Hull, the revels would be shared by Jolyneddy and his jovial teamsters.

One figure, little noticed, goes amongst them. He is the Dan Chaucer of the village, seeing all and saying little. What he made of Aptrick Fair was told in random verse ; and the stuff of it, if not the literary strength, was akin to Chaucer's own. Canterbury, after all, never had a monopoly of pilgrims or of minstrels. Each day of the fair ended with country dances, and on the third night there was a play at the High Hall. The Dale always had a passion for the drama, and a true gift of interpretation, and from the seventeenth century onwards its heart was given to Shakespeare.

One would give much to go back—not in fancy, but reality— to an evening such as bygone times saw once a year at the Hall. The Aptrick men and maidens took the wide Minstrel Gallery as their stage. Buckskin breeches, a long, stiff coat and buckled shoes were *de rigueur* for the hero, whatever play was acted. The heroine, no doubt, wore just what her mirror counselled.

Below, the neighbouring gentry, their wives and daughters, sat in the shadowed hall, with its pleasant odour of bees-waxed oak and smouldering logs. Above, candles guttered in their sconces while Othello was making an end of Desdemona, and the village scene-shifter came on unabashed in his workaday shepherd's smock to replace old lights with new. It did not matter. The play was the thing, and downright, honest acting carried all before it.

Then afterwards the dining hall was cleared. Actors and gentry danced Robin-a-hedge together, and many another measure, to the music of fiddlers seated in the Minstrel Gallery. And after that the stirrup-cups, the ripe, October air blowing soft through Aptrick from Simon's Seat as the players drifted out into the night. They went through a village whose every other house wore a branch of oak or ash above its door. If there was a moon, its mellow light showed the breeze-stirred leafage; if not, a stable-lanthorn served its place. And here at once they were in touch with Shakespeare's England. One of them might lately have been declaiming from the Minstrel Gallery that "good wine needs no bush"—and here in Aptrick's very street were the bushes that made each house a tavern for as long as the fair lasted.

Shakespeare's strong, insistent hold on the Dale, almost to our own day, seems scarcely to need explanation. He was sincere and loyal to himself. He fed genius on his own home-country— on the lives of usual men who shared his everydays, and on the life that stirred among the meadows and the woodland streams of Warwickshire. And so his work found answer—needs must —in the hearts of countrymen throughout the English land.

Close to Aptrick, too, is an amphitheatre that has waited patiently throughout the centuries for the lads and lasses to stage there "A Midsummer Night's Dream." Few know the place. You reach it from the village street by way of a mistal-yard and a pasture field. Then, without warning, the track strides into a place so silent, so primitive, that one halts in sheer astonishment. Great walls of rock encircle it, sheer to the sky. No wind stirs, and few birds sing. Blackthorn and dwarf scrub beard the rock-foot, stretching to the marshes where Enchanter's Nightshade grows. And in the middle of this desolation lies a carpet of greensward, rich and soft, cropped close by vagrant sheep.

The elm at the lane-top.

The Grecian Court would have to find precarious seats among the rocks, if they were minded to look on at the play. That is their affair. For myself, I could get the strolling players to my hand, and send them here without undue rehearsal of their parts. Bottom the Weaver lives not far away. He is for ever wanting to "play Thisbe, too," or indeed any part. The other rustics are all within easy hail. What a play it would be, in such a setting, and with such actors! Puck would not need to be told of the adventure. He would come of his own accord, from a fairy-haunted land where little is doing in these days of merchantry for money's sake. Titania would wake from her long sleep, winking the dewdrops away from starry eyes; and Oberon would get himself a new costume for the play, bidding the fairy-loomsters hurry with their weaving.

If you can get away from that enchanted hollow—a hard thing to do—and climb the rock-face by help of a kindly sapling here and there—you come straight into the bare lands bordering Greenhow. The solitary acres have no thought of Titania and her revels. They are fighting to give livelihood to their children —the bleak, complaining sheep, the curlews, and the hoody crows—and have enough to do, God knows. Yet cross the barren lands, and turn down the green track that was ancient when the Romans came among us, and again you find the sheltered valley and the Aptrick Road. The lane crosses the highway here and goes down to the pleasant farmstead known as Woodhouse. Again the sense of great antiquity is with one. The elm at the lane-top is incalculably old. The house below is the only remnant of a thriving village whose foundations now lie deep under pasture soil. It brings no surprise to know that a most curious haunting survives along this farm-lane.

Those who speak seldom of it, just because they have seen and know, say that a man's figure accompanies you as you go down to Woodhouse. He walks step by step with you in the field on the left hand ; and the fence between is so high that only his head and shoulders can be seen. A grey, stern face he turns to you, and eyes sombre with reproach. He goes as far as the lane-foot, then suddenly you find yourself alone. One may smile at such superstitions to-day, in the merry sunlight that makes a playground of the Aptrick Road. But pass that way in the chill of a November gloaming, and the " other-sense " may creep from the ever-waiting past to stifle unbelief.

The Aptrick Road is a winding track. Few yards are straight or level. The first architects of it, I think, were drovers lazying behind sheep and cattle that turned this way and that to nibble at tempting clumps of herbage. A track was formed, growing wider by degrees. Then the first road-maker arrived. He was suspected in his day of being a dare-devil fellow, full of ideas beyond what was good or proper, but he was so far wedded to tradition that he built his road precisely as the drovers—or their cattle, rather—had mapped it out already. That is the English way, and we survive long after Rome and her legions, with their ruthless mathematics of straight, unswerving roads, have gone to dust and classic burial. The Aptrick Road is an English highway still, unfit for speedy traffic; and its banks are bordered by deep grass and wildflowers, by legends thick as black-berries in a kindly fruiting season.

An English highway, unfit for speedy traffic

You take a hill or two, and a dip, and find yourself at Hart-lington, where the little bridge goes over Dibble River. It is another haunted corner of the Dale—haunted by a most exquis-ite and melodious peace. The hollow lies so deeply sheltered that it has a climate of its own, and in February you may find stray flowers in bloom that have not dared to bud as yet outside these charmed boundaries. The wheel of the old water-mill above is humming a cheery roundelay. The stream, brown and swift, has its own song as it swings under the grey arch; and the words of the song are yours, if you have traced it from its source on the lean highlands.

Not far above, Dibble River is no more than a beck, scolding its way between dour stones and boulders. Then its banks grow steeper and more wooded, till part of its growing flood goes by a ferny way of its own to the little lake that feeds the mill-wheel. No words can explain the beauty of that lake, its lush abandonment to all that sheltered warmth can do. The trees, wide-branched and silent, gaze at themselves in a mirror starred with water-flowers. One waits, somehow, breathless and expectant, for Elaine's barge of death to steal over the hushed

The little bridge

waters. One almost hears Lancelot and Guinevere the Queen whispering together in the woodland, and feels Merlin's spirit brooding in the sunlit air. It is as if Lyonesse and the soft West Country had sent its heart for a sojourn in our rough and forth-right highlands. Yet the stream's other part, separated at the ferny way, goes down into a gorge of wildness and of tumult. Its floods have bared gaunt roots of trees, and the flotsam lies piled in heedless disarray among the cliffs. Here at the quiet bridge the divided currents mingle and are one again; and the song of Dibble Water is all made up of parting and lone adventures and gladness in reunion.

The trouble on this road is to get away from one enchant-ment to the next, as if a man had twenty pleasant life-times instead of only one. A little way on, at the crest of the rise, there's a wayside well whose history I would give much to know. Not the vaguest of traditions is left to suggest who chiselled its message deep into the stone. The pity is that he chose Latin for the inscription. Translated into sound English, it runs, " Let the horse drink at the spring, and thereafter lift his head with joy." Once I found an ancient wayfarer standing at the well. He turned a puzzled face to me, and asked what the foreign lingo meant. His face lit up when I explained.

" Why couldn't the fellow put it plain ? " he asked. " I'd always a fondness for horses myself, and it was a good sort of thought, say I."

Sir William Craven joins company with one again further on. But for him, there would have been no bridge across the Wharfe in James the First's time. The foundations are of his day ; but Wharfe in her headlong floods has wrecked the arches more than once. The Burnsall and Aptrick men were cradled in wind-gusts and storm ; and they built the arches up again, each time stronger than before. Burnsall Bridge, as it stands to-day, is a great prose-poem, instinct in its stones with all that the north-bred temper means. For long years the bridge is there to cross by, accepted as a usual matter ; but let Wharfe rive it down, and all the township is sturdy to rebuild it—not for convenience only, but from a deeper motive of half-religious love for every bridge that strides running water.

It is from the bridge here that Burnsall's yearly contest begins and finishes. She keeps the great tradition of the Fell Race alive, and as a classic it is second only to the Guides' Race. The Lakeland runners come to it, indeed, and none who watched the going in what is still remembered as " Dalzell's Year " can forget the breathless venture. The course is long and punishing.

It goes up the pastures first, that seem steep till the further moor is reached—the moor that climbs sheer to the sky-line over wiry heather, boulder-strewn.

As a spectacle, the scene has no equal. The bridge's parapet is thronged with eager watchers. So is the village green, and all the strip of roadway leading to the pastures. To the left of the wide amphitheatre sweep the Barden pine-woods and the high fells raking up to Simon's Seat. In front are the climbing figures, small against the moor's swart background. When the

An up-Dale bridge

runners reach the turning-post at last, they are limned thin as pencils against a sky that seems to dwarf their epic combat.

A Fell Race, of all contests, is the most exacting. It asks for so many kinds of endurance, for judgment and the big heart to prevail—and for a full measure of good luck in the descent. To go at speed up testing slopes, and yet to nurse one's wind—to cross the bumpy, wind-swept tops that lead to the turning-post—to hurl one's self down-moor, all out for speed whatever happens in the way of hidden boulders or the snare of tricky marshes—these ask for a peculiar courage, a hardihood that few enjoy. Why, else, are there so few entrants for the Guides' Race, or for ours here at Burnsall ? The prestige attaching to these two north-country Marathons is worth any hale man's winning. If more had strength for the adventure, there would be a mob of entrants; but these two races remain, now as of old, a high test of endurance for stalwarts who are few.

Somehow one hopes that William Craven returned from the Further Lands to watch Dalzell run that magical race of his. It would have heartened Craven's self-same type of pluck to see him stride up the pastures to the moor—cross the skyline—come hurtling down with wind in his hefty feet. He was not running merely, or leaping, or sliding over treacherous ground. He was doing all three at once, in some astounding way, and his gait suggested the antelope's, slim, care-free, swift as the footless wind. Another may come in our time to lower his amazing record; but he will need to be hefty and hard-bitten.

Whether William Craven watched that race or no, he is with us now as we leave the bridge and take the road through Burnsall village. Now, as in Craven's time, it is a village favoured by the gods. Peace and dignity have settled here. Its inn, long-fronted, quiet, and unobtrusive, is of the olden tavern breed, designed for hospitality and men's content. Barden's great pine-woods stride down almost to the green, and the fells are ranged in high companies, sentries of its restful ease. Our northern Dick Whittington still goes with us as we idle up the road. It was he who founded the school that stands as in his day, its every grey stone left to teach us how truly the Elizabethans knew how to build. Though it was reared in early Stuart days, Sir William was conservative in architecture; and they say that Burnsall school is the finest building of its type to survive in England. One of the Dale's priceless heritages, it seems remote from to-day, and when modern school hours are over, the old walls talk together, one fancies, of the times when they were young, and the dominie told his urchins how a great fleet named the Armada had gone sprawling, wrecked and doomed, along the British coasts.

Just above the school is the kirkyard, with its folk who have gone into the further lands, its lychgate, and the church comely with centuries of worship. And across the highway is a fine yeoman's house, its back to the road, in token that it was built when every substantial homestead was fortified in self-defence. Burnsall, cradled in a hollow that poets might dream of, was usual, then as now, so far as three things went—need

The hills' brooding peace

of worship, of a man's strength to keep his house against marauders, of teaching for his children. And out of these three, one fancies, has been bred the sufficing strength that Burnsall gives one always in times of stress. Her peace, hard won and thrifty, is not of yesterday. It has gladdened at the mystery of spring and leafing buds, laughed with summer and its pride, has sorrowed through the centuries at many graves. And still her heart is wise, and kind, and youthful, though she's old.

The road forward is to many hearts a glamoured way, for it leads to Thorpe-sub-Montem, as old maps have the name—to little Thorpe-in-the-Hollow, as her lovers think of her. Folk come for the first time to Thorpe and try to explain her magic.

Afterwards they cease that attempt. There are things felt and known that are like the air of a happy, wordless song.

One sprightly tale links Burnsall left behind with Thorpe to come. Once on a day the Burnsall villagers reared a Maypole on their green. It was a fine pole, and perhaps they aired their pride too freely. At any rate, it was there in place one autumn evening ; and the next day it had gone. The news spread fast, and a great company gathered about the hole in the ground that witnessed to the robbery. Wat Truelove, the village wiseacre, made a speech. He opined—and pressed the point home fluently—that there were many he could name in Burnsall whose lives suggested traffic with the Evil One. There had been three thunderstorms last week, each worse than t'other, and that alone proved it. And now the devil had flown away with the Maypole.

Andrew Turner raised a laugh by declaring that Old Nick had no liking for such innocent affairs as dancing round a Maypole ; and the brawny smith suggested, with blunt common-sense, that the Aptrick men were always up to some cantrip or another.

" Lads will allus be lads," he ended. " They never grow up, out Aptrick way."

He had the ear of the meeting at once, and a wrathful band set out for Aptrick. They tried Barden next, and Hebden, and roamed to Linton. The more the story got abroad, the richer grew jest and banter of their neighbours. It was a wide country, doubtless ; but, after all, a Maypole was not a bauble to be tucked away in a man's pocket. Nobody thought of little Thorpe, till on the second day they were going over-fell to Cracoe in maddened search, and one of them glanced down into the hamlet far below and saw the tapered end of their pole gleaming in the sunlight. They went like one disgruntled man into Thorpe Hollow, and the tale of what happened has many variants ; but the version that is most likeable is also truest to the Dale spirit.

The Burnsall men, it seems, came roaring down and massed themselves about the pole.   The Thorpe cobblers ran from every house, and asked what was to do.

" Enough and to spare," said the Burnsall blacksmith, with his coat off and his muscles showing plainly—muscles as big as Simon's Seat, or near thereby, one chronicler relates.

" Best be out with your trouble, then."

The smith was stuttering with rage by this time.

" Is this our Maypole, or isn't it, you flea-pricked cobblers ? "

" How should we say ?   We never wanted flimsies—May Queens and trash o' that sort—and Thorpe was puzzled when she woke to find somebody had dropped your pole where it wasn't asked or needed."

That began the fight, and the end of it was not at once.   It was a great combat, clean as English fists could make it.   And afterwards, with honours equally divided, they rested from toil and consumed together a hogshead of ale broached in the open. This ritual finished, the Thorpe and Burnsall men shouldered the cause of all the tumult and planted the Maypole deep and firm again in its old home.   It is a good tale to have for company along the road to Thorpe.

XI

THORPE-IN-THE-HOLLOW

The Cobblers of Thorpe—The Devil's Bridge—Gabriel's Hounds—Dan Waddilove—The Cobblers' Tapping.

OF all the hamlets nestling in the Dale's secret places, Thorpe is the most hidden and most winsome. Peace broods at her heart. The winds are quiet here, the houses old and kindly. One knows it somehow to be haunted only by good memories—a sanctuary, saved through the wear and tear of centuries to give rest to tired wayfarers. It was a sanctuary once in stark earnest. The Scots swept raiding down, to Skipton or to Bolton Priory. Right in the fork between these two tracks lay Thorpe, and the women hid themselves here with the children and the cattle, while their men went out to fight. And not once were they surprised.

Four tracks lead into Thorpe nowadays ; yet she lies so snug in her hollow that a man might travel any of these ways, and stand almost in sight of her roofs, and yet see nothing but the fells, the moors, the bleak and savage highlands bordering Greenhow on the Hill. It is the same story always through the Dale, this love of the man-lands for their girl-children. They take the storms' onsets, and shoulder them off with a laugh, protecting such bairns as Thorpe-in-the-Hollow.

The hamlet was once a busy hive of cobblers. There was no stint of work in those days, for they had the custom of Fountains Abbey, a sure and steady market ; though why the monks there should be dependent on Thorpe for the shoeing of their feet will always be a mystery. Thirty miles or so of hilly country divided them, by the shortest track over the tops. The cobblers' burdens of mended shoes on the outward journey and shoes to mend on the return, could not be light. But it is history—and romance—that they took those constant journeys.

A jolly race, these shoemakers, as they emerge from the mists of old-time story. They worked well and played well; and

The winds are quiet here, the houses old and kindly

constantly the most diverting things happened to them on their journey home from Fountains. Their adventures, though chronicled still when tongues wag beside cosy hearths, may be counted as old wives' tales in a literal sense—tales recounted to their wives when they returned the worse for wear from the many taverns on the homeward track.

There was Ralph Calvert. He could sole three pairs of shoes, they say, while another man had scarce finished two. A little and a nimble man—hands and feet and wits all quick together—

he was a prime favourite at the Abbey and in every place where men forgathered. Small wonder that his holidays were ripe and boisterous, or that at the end of the tramp from Fountains he would return to Thorpe with a look about him that his good wife knew by heart. Ralph would set down his pack gravely, as soon as he came into his cottage, and would count the tally.

" Two pairs of the Abbot's—good and holy feet, if a trifle large—and a pair belonging to the Almoner. He wears 'em down, slip-shod like ; I'd know 'em anywhere."

So he would count them, soberly and well, till he had placed all the monks' shoes in a row and added to them others brought home to mend from many a wayside farm. And he knew the owner of each pair, just by the way he had worn the leather, as well as he knew the man's face. Then he would put business out of mind, and sit down to supper, and let his tongue wag, like Ulysses of old on similar occasions, about the wild adventures that had beset him on the road.

One of these tales was so deftly spun, indeed, that it finds belief to-day among the elders. It is bold and picturesque in outline, and concerns what happened to Ralph at Dibble Bridge on the road home from Fountains. The place itself is wild enough to father any legend ; for the bleak track from Pateley strides into a ravine so sheltered and so dumb that one misses the wind's friendly piping which chilled one on the higher lands. The stream, too, goes thin and silent except in times of heavy rain ; and sunlight can do little to redeem its stark and utter loneliness. Ralph Calvert, as he told the story, explained how he came with his pack to the ravine. There was no bridge then across the stream, but a ford that at this season of the year he expected to cross dry-shod. Instead, the flood was wading deep ; and he crossed at hazard, his feet stumbling on hidden boulders. When he came to the far side, the sun was getting down. Weary for home as he was, he fell asleep. He was roused by a gentle shaking, and found a stranger looking down on him.

" Eh ? " growled Ralph.

" I heard you talking in your sleep," said the stranger pleasantly. " You longed for a bridge to be built over Dibble Water. You'd taken a wetting as you crossed, and didn't want another the next time you came this way."

" That's true enough to my dreams, though I didn't know I'd said as much aloud."

" You can have the bridge at your pleasure."

" Can I ? " asked the cobbler warily. " A man seldom gets much for striving, and naught at all for the simple asking."

" Do you want the bridge, Ralph Calvert ? "

" Nay, I'm not particular either way. But who are you to build it ? "

The stranger then disclosed his station, but Ralph was sceptical though awed a little.

" Meaning no disrespect," he ventured, " you've neither horns nor tail."

" Dear bumpkin," laughed the other pleasantly, " I never had."

So then, as Ralph told the story to his wife, " they gat to business." The Devil proposed to build him a bridge across the stream on the simple condition that he should have the soul of the first living thing to cross its arch ; and all the man in Calvert rose in hot revolt.

" I'll make no mucky bargain—but I'll fight," said he.

They wrestled, stark and long, till the adversary threw Ralph at last, and picked him up and patted him on the shoulder.

" So few stand up to me, cobbler," he said, with a tired, quiet laugh, " and I'll build your bridge without any price at all."

Ralph finished his tale, and his wife glanced at him with exasperating sympathy.

" To be sure, it's a far step home from Fountains, and the day's warm, and all. I don't wonder you fell asleep and had queer dreams."

Yet the next day news spread like wildfire that Dibble Water was bridged. A high arch of stone, trimly built, spanned the flooded stream, and none knew how it came there.

The legend is unique, so far as one knows. In all others of the kind the Prince of Darkness makes his bargain, and means to stick to it. He is robbed of his due by subtlety. A dog is the first to cross, or a heifer, or a sow. The stratagem leaves one cold, as when Shylock was fobbed off by a legal quibble when he asked his pound of flesh. But here all is fair dealing, and this bridge is constantly a reminder that even the Devil ought to have his due. Once, at any rate, he showed himself a good loser and true sportsman.

Ralph Calvert had no monopoly of queer happenings. Another cobbler lost his way from Fountains once. Dark overtook him, as he came into Troller's Ghyll, by way of one of the oldest foot-tracks in the Dale, but soon a full moon rose above the tattered skein of cloud. And first he heard a scud of hoofs, and saw the Ghostly Hunt go by—men on winged horses, chasing for ever the souls of bairns who died unbaptized. It was known to him as the Gabble-Ratchet; and in the forefront of the hunt were Gabriel's Hounds, slim and long-bodied, hurtling through the upper moonlight in hot pursuit. These passed, and as he stood there, wet with panic, a running whine came down the Ghyll. Gabriel's Hounds were far above him; but all men knew that Barguest had his lair on earth in this same Troller's Ghyll. And presently the dog came out into the moonlight—" big as a littlish bear," as the lost wayfarer passed on the tale, " and yellow, with great eyes like saucers. He'd a shaggy sort o' smell as he went by, and I counted myself for dead. But he chanced not to glimpse me, praise all the saints that ever were."

There was Daniel Waddilove, too, who lost himself on Elboton one moonlit night and fell among the fairies. The name itself means " Elves Hill," and of all places in the Dale, except Barden, this is the fullest of rich, persistent fairy-lore. If the Little People are dead and out of mind, as they assure us, ask the doubters who else make the mushroom-rings that grace its slopes ? Dan Waddilove, it seems, had " got across " with one of the elf-tribe, and so of course the whole race was at feud with him. And what happened to him is a tale packed full of whimsical, affrighting matters. The Fairy Queen let Puck loose on him ; and all that night he was following " corpsie-lights " that led him into boggy ground, or fancying a dog bit him on the calf, or listening to the shrieks of witches as they rode overhead on flying broomsticks. Dan experienced, in fact, all that one sib to the fairies escaped, as a wiser man had once eluded havoc in Barden's russet, night-time forest. But at the end of all the Queen beckoned him to come forward and kiss hands.

" Mock us no more, and go free," she said.

And Dan always finished the tale with a sigh. " She'd a voice like a lile, silver trumpet ; and I wish I could hear it again."

Thorpe-in-the-Hollow cradles such old tales. They are part of the quiet hamlet, inwoven with the lowing of its kine, the bark of sheep dogs, the lusty reek of mistals. They are a farming people to-day, and husbandry brings peace of heart and soul. So does memory, linked arm in arm with many yesterdays.

Lest I be thought altogether a praiser of the living past, let me tell the great adventure that once met me on the road to Thorpe. It was June, with a hot sun overhead, and I overtook a man, obviously of the towns. He carried a heavy-looking bag.

" Am I right for Thorpe ? " he asked.

" So right that you're almost there."

We went up the hill together, and halted at that wonderful corner where the moors and the high fells stand guardians to the hamlet. The stranger stood looking at it all, like a man who had wandered far in search of well-worth-while and had found it.

"I'm from Northampton, you see," he went on presently—"in the boot trade, and travelling for custom. Northampton seems a far way off, somehow."

The man was lost in some sufficing dream. It stayed with

Where the moors and high fells stand guardians to the hamlet

him as we went down the hill and through the hamlet, drowsing in the sunlight.

"You can almost hear 'em tapping," he said at last—"the cobblers, I mean."

Then he unburdened himself. He had read a great deal about the shoemakers of Thorpe, till a picture of it took firm shape and became the companion of his days. Going about his business there in Northampton, he had let fancy roam about the might-have-been of this secluded hamlet. The modern boot-trade might have grown to full stature here, till street was added to mean street, and factories belched their smoke, and pinched-faced newsboys ran about with tidings of " all the winners." My companion of an hour left me with a memory that abides. From all that he said and left unsaid, I knew that he had stolen away from the weariness of trade to find some soul of poetry within the leather industry. Romance he must have, to keep heart alive ; and he found it, in this sanctuary where neighbourly, kind breezes steal from the moor about the blue wood-reek from clustered chimney stacks.

He missed full hearing when he said that you could *almost* hear the cobblers' tapping. Thorpe's intimates, choosing the right hour, can always hear that music. It comes out of the night and the silence. The rooks are asleep overhead. Owls have done with their hunting for awhile. Faint and low at first, it grows in volume till the whole, deep hollow is filled with hammer-taps. The tapping changes soon to the lilt of a marching song, as the cobblers get over-hill to Fountains with their packs. There's laughter, and frolic, and heartsease— tang o' the wind as it meets them on the tops—and in between some haphazard note of chanted litanies that will meet them later on at Fountains.

It is good that such memoried hamlets still keep their peace inviolate. Thorpe is beyond praise, or thought of it. She is the queen-lady of the Dale's villages. And if you ask me why, I say because she's Thorpe. And that, I take it, is simple, heart-whole love.

XII

LINTON THREE BRIDGES

*Richard Fountaine—Undertaker-in-Chief in the Great Plague—
"Strike, Daykin, the Devil's in the Hemp"—A Foundling of the
Dales—A Hard-Bitten Dalesman.*

FROM Thorpe to Linton-in-Craven is a short and pleasant
journey, whether you take it by field-tracks or the highway; and at its ending you find a place of singular repose
and charm. When one has lived long in a village, with faithful
caring, it is hard to disentangle the many threads of memory
that make her what she is. Romance of her many legends
mingles with glamoured moments of the past—the first true
day of spring, with cock-throstles up in the sycamores and the
rooks assembled for a great nursery inspection—October
gloamings, nutty-sweet and touched by frost, when one has
swung home after a day's shooting up the pasture or the moor,
the game-bag heavy and the body aching with a big, contented
weariness—neighbours who have shared those intimacies of
give-and-take which are the salt of country life—all have been
woven so long ago into the pattern that it is hard to say where
anything begins or ends in this astounding passion for one's
homeland.

Linton, compact about its stream, is spanned by three bridges
that in themselves are landmarks of its story. First the wide
bridge, carrying wheeled traffic that forty years ago forded
Linton Beck for lack of other means to cross it. Then the slim,
narrow arch, graceful in its strength as the century that saw it

built. And higher up again, the great slabs of stone, without parapets or thought of such protection—slabs worn into ruts by the feet of many generations before Linton asked for any more elaborate crossing. About these bridges and the village green the cottages and farmsteads are gathered close together— so close, and arranged so queerly to the modern view, that one reason only seems to explain their builders' minds. The same reason bade Skipton build her " yards." The Scots were busy along the Dale in the days of Linton's youth.

Linton's oldest bridge

The modest inn bears the sign of " The Fountaine Arms," and above the oldest bridge of all stands what is known as " The Hospital"—a massive building, with an orderly, paved court-yard in front of its eight little houses and their private chapel. The high fells show above its chimneys, dwarfing its pride to true proportion. There is little remembered now in the village of the connection between Richard Fountaine, whose name stands over the inn, and the Hospital. Yet the story is sheer romance, of the sort that Defoe would have loved to handle when he was busy with the London plague.

Fountaine went to London Town to seek his fortune, like many another. Unlike most, he found it, and prospered as a timber merchant and undertaker. Then the plague came, and the city lay in stifled dread. To take the plague was to die of it, except by a rare miracle. The folk perished. Many who still lived were groaning in agony behind closed doors—doors with the warning plague-mark on them—or were trundling hearse-carts through the streets. Brave priests were entering stricken houses, to give the last consolation ; and in all the city these alone sought bright-eyed for the warning cross that others shunned. It is hard to get down, in imagination, to the bed-rock of those times. The plague walked in silence absolute. London had known assaults enough from human foes who yelled their battle-cries, and slew, and spared not. But it had been fight with a seen enemy—fight that allowed quick, answering blows, and wounded more than ever it killed. The plague was at each man's elbow, invisible ; and, where three recovered, ninety-and-seven found the death that was respite from appalling agony.

Richard Fountaine took it, and won through. Thin and grey-faced, he went about the streets again, immune from the dread that quickened the steps of most passers-by. His name came to the ears of a distracted Government, and they made him Undertaker-in-Chief to the city—a grim appointment, rendered grimmer still by the patronage his trade as a timber merchant brought him. Most of the dead were hurried into plague-pits and smothered with loads of quick-lime. But those in high places naturally preferred more decent obsequies for their kin, and they turned to Fountaine, now High Undertaker, to provide private graves. Their fees were handsome.

Along this drear, macabre route Fountaine plied his trade, and built a great fortune up. One does not judge him. In all wars the lust of gain seems to spring new-born, side by side with the lust to die for no gain at all except honour. And that war of the Great Pestilence against London must have been a staggering onset for any man to stand against, and all but die, and afterwards recover. It must indeed have made him gluttonous for wealth—for what it could bring him as recompense for standing on the brink of death. Some measure of Richard Fountaine's heart and mind, when riches came, is given by his will. In his native place of Linton-in-Craven, and in the Essex village where he settled after the Great Fire had cleansed the city, he willed that Hospitals should be built, each to accommodate poor and decent people of their respective parishes. There must be a chapelry in

Graceful in its strength as the century that saw it built

each of these alms-places, and services by the parish priest on two days of the week, the said priest to have his proper dues and moneys. And this in thankfulness to God for his recovery from the plague and the after blessings that accrued. A singular life-story, echoed down the generations when the chapel bell rings still for its two weekly services. Do they know the tale, one wonders, in the Essex village where the twin-sister of our Hospital stands—feature by feature alike, the two of them built from the same architect's plan?

Linton is honeycombed with legends. Its fields and

coppices are full of half-forgotten lore and curious hauntings. To live long in its companionship is to be aware that the past is strong here, tenacious of its memories, lying in wait always for the friendly soul to pass who cares for bygone days. The lane that goes between the Hospital and the grey, clustered home-steads takes you into a waste of low-lying fields, drained by a soft-flowing stream. These boggy acres seem to have nothing to tell, except that they yield a rare harvest of snipe to the gun. Yet out of them was born the oddest family motto known to the Heralds' College.

There was a wide lake here once—haunt of gull and wild-duck and lesser water-fowl—and bordering it the flax-fields stretched far out to the rising ground towards Thorpe and Threaplands. One can only imagine what the time of flax-flowering must have shown to men alive in those times : acre on acre, nothing but swaying billows of blue haze, so that the sunlight dancing with the breeze caught up the blue into its gold. Above it all, the green, steep slope of Elboton Hill, where the fairies play by night ; and over that again the rough, swart moors, for ever guarding their cherished lowlands.

Giles Daykin lived then at Linton Hall—the house old in strength and dignity that is the last outpost of the village on the Skipton Road—and his interest in flax began when the flowering time was done. Hemp was its country name, and it was building a fortune for Daykin, without ever a need to tramp to London Town in search of riches.

The legend takes shape first in the tavern bought long after-wards by Richard Fountaine and renamed by him. Two strangers sat drinking their rum and talked of Daykin's out-buildings, filled with the year's flax-crop just harvested. They spoke, too, of a little door connecting one of these store-houses with the house itself, and of the substantial sums in gold that Daykin kept in his big, four-poster bed. A bed in those days was a wooden fortress, closed by a sliding panel when the goodman climbed up for hard-won slumber. Within its roomy bulk were other panels, hiding cupboards where his treasure lay. He slept with what he earned, and, when he rose for the day's business, he closed the outer panel on it and left all secure.

Old Boniface Platts, who kept the inn, was drowsing by the peat fire. Twice one of the strangers had to shout in his ear when he and his crony were needing liquor. And twice, after he had served them, he settled into his chair again, and snored with the thin, reedy softness of old age. There's none so fast asleep as he who stays awake to listen. One of the men expounded his simple plan. He meant to wait for dusk, and then creep softly to the outhouse and hide himself among the hemp.

"He keeps a blunderbuss inside that bed of his," said his crony.

"Ay, but dursn't let it off! The last time he fired it—from his window, at me—it hit him backward-like, and I only got a dollop o' lead through the top of my thick head."

Gloaming filtered soft and rosy through the window, and then grey night settled down about the village. The two strangers roused the landlord, paid their score, and went out into the dark.

The old innkeeper showed no sign of slumber now. He straddled his glowing hearth, and glanced at the door from time to time in great perplexity. Daykin had always stood his friend in lean times and prosperous. Boniface's impulse was to warn him of the plot. Yes, but the two strangers, he supposed, belonged to the numerous race of tinkers, and to injure one was to make enemies of all for life. There was little the tinkers could not do to a man, once their feud was up against him— stealthy, quiet hindrances that broke his spirit if they left his body whole. Boniface Platts was no coward, but a younger man might well have left the matter where it stood, arguing that Daykin must look after himself, as others had to do. Platts tried that argument without avail. *Daykin had always stood his friend*—the words kept singing in his ears. He went out at last. A soft greyness lit the road for him after his eyes grew used to the night, and he crossed to Linton Manor. Daykin himself, as it happened, had just returned from Skipton. He was getting down from his horse when Platts crept out of the gloom.

" Lord, how you startled me ! " growled the horseman. " What d'ye want of me this time, Boniface ? "

" *Strike, Daykin, the devil's in the hemp*," quavered the inn-keeper.

" You've been at your own cellar, man. What can I make of such moonshine talk as that ? "

So then Platts whispered in his ear, and crept back to his inn, and double-bolted his door. It was natural that his inbred fear of the tinkers should set imagination working, so that reprisal seemed to be following almost at his heels. He had told his tale, but a right conscience is often slow to bring its true reward of courage.

Daykin himself had no superstition touching the tinkers. He went into his house and listened at the door of the out-building—to know if Platts had spoken truth—and heard the two gypsies chattering quietly in their hiding-place among the flax. Then he went quietly out, through Linton village, rousing the hale men. They took the skulking thieves and stripped them mother-naked, tarred and feathered them for decency's sake, and sped them into the wilderness.

That is the simpler legend. The other, more widely-known among the older generations of Linton folk, is so thick with detail that one can hardly see the wood for the trees. Boniface Platts figures in it, but not as a prime actor. His tavern is the scene of a great deal of talk and counter-talk as to the meaning of a strange message that has been brought to Giles Daykin by a mysterious horseman with a gypsy look about him. Each of the company has his own prolix view as to the meaning of, " Strike, Daykin, the devil is in the hemp," till opinion settles down at last to the plain issue that thieves are lurking in Daykin's barn. The whole village, in this version of the tale, is made privy to the affair, and waits behind darkened windows for the signal that the marauders are taken.

The story of their capture is long drawn-out and full of details that confuse each other ; but again the finish emerges, as in the simpler legend. Three thieves are taken in this version, instead of two. The mysterious horseman, who delivered the message earlier in the day, reappears and announces himself as Johnnie Faa, of the gypsy clan spread wide from Carlisle to the Dale. Mr. Daykin, he explains, had ever been kind to the gypsies when others persecuted them ; and the Faas have long memories for both sorts of treatment. He then takes charge of what he names, " Jedburgh court of law," whose guiding precept is to hang first and try the culprit afterwards for form's sake. The villagers are crowding now round the stable-yard of Daykin's house, and help in the pleasant pastime of hanging the first of the three vagabonds. Johnnie Faa relents as to the two others. They are but lads, and he sentences them only to be ducked in the stream, tarred and feathered, and then let go their ways.

In detail again the second version of the tale is at variance with the first. They cannot find enough feathers to coat the brawny lads, so Faa asks if there's wool to be had in a sheep-growing dale. A great shout of laughter rises, and by-and-by the two who have found mercy at the hands of Jedburgh Law go out, tarred and wooled, into the night.

A diverting and altogether picturesque addition to the story tells of how a shepherd, coming from the fells next morning, encountered two fearsome beasts, reared on their hind-legs and moaning piteously.

" Like as you might say a couple of Barguests, but stranger than the usual," he would say—" and, lordie, how I ran ! "

In essentials the tales agree ; and the gist of them was embodied by Giles Daykin's son—settled in London, and a High Sheriff later on—in the odd motto, " Stryke, Daykin, the devil's in the hemp."

The owls are hooting, as I sit here, with a pen that has taken the lead and wanders where it lists with memories. We were ever " behind the times " in Linton Three Bridges—in touch with better ones from our own point of view—and it is not many years since an immemorial custom was in vogue at the Fountaine Inn. " Old Mary," of quiet and pleasant memory, was the landlady there, and on each side of the hearth was an oak chair, with a churchwarden pipe on the wall above it. One chair and pipe were appropriated to the Squire of Linton, who lived just beyond what had once been Daykin's house ; the other to Christopher Dean, a yeoman born of yeomen whose ancestry went back to Elizabethan days. Whoever chanced to be sitting in one or other of the chairs must yield it if its proper tenant entered ; and the Squire and Christopher would sit together on many an evening, discussing to-morrow's weather or the tales of centuries long dead. Shepherds and farmers—a travelling tinker, maybe, stumping in to join the company— would put in a slow jest now and then. And Mary, with her wrinkled, kindly face, would stand and watch them all. They were guests of her tavern, rather than money bringers ; and if her ale was ripe and nutty, so was her outlook upon men and life.

This Christopher Dean, yeoman of an ancient line, lived at the farmstead just outside my gate. He went out on a blithe day near the end of June to begin the hay mowing—early that year—

and found a basket in his porch. Inside the basket was a month-old baby, and Christopher, recovered a little from the shock, called for his wife.

" What is it ? " she answered from the kitchen. " I'm thrang and busy."

" You'll be busier by-and-by, if I know aught."

So Mistress Dean bustled into the porch, and looked from Christopher to the basket, and back again at his awed face.

" I found it waiting in the porch," said he.

" Well, it's not lighted gunpowder, is it ? "

And with that, as Christopher told the happening later on, " she fair swooped down on the babby, and crooned and laughed o'er it, and cried in between. Then her face went all like a flint. ' The hussy,' said she. ' And nay,' said I, ' that's a hard name to give one that cannot have earned it yet. And, besides, it might be a lad, for all we know. A lad may be twenty things, but you couldn't call him a hussy.' "

His wife explained with scorn that of course no man could ever be expected to know he'd got the bonniest girl-bairn in the Dale under his roof. When she spoke of a hussy, she was thinking of the babe's mother, who could leave such a tender lamb to anybody else's caring. And, talking of lambs, he was constable of the parish and answerable for strayed sheep and such-like.

Christopher Dean was indeed the constable, in the old meaning that survived in Linton like the two chairs in the inn, set there for Squire and yeoman ; an office of the heart, without other reward than pleasure in getting about his neighbours' business when it needed his shrewd wisdom and kindly judgment. So, while the goodwife fussed indoors about the foundling—and came near to believing that, after all these years, she had another of her own, hard won through travail—the yeoman went up and down the village, telling the simple need of money to rear up the babe.

The Squire was good for a yearly tribute. So was Christopher Dean. So were all the farmer-folk, according to their means. Between them they reared the foundling to shy, graceful womanhood, till a strapping farmer came over the tops from Yoredale and never rested till he'd won her to his own good home. She was so bonny. That was his first thought of her—and his last, when he died with her hand in his.

If one were concerned with writing a novel, instead of with plain happenings that gather round one from the elder days, what mysteries would attend that basket left in the farmstead porch. There would be a coronet at least on the babe's linen—linen of a quality and texture hitherto unknown in Linton parish. And the child would have been left by no " hussy," but by a great and sorely-tried lady whose husband was banished for allegiance to some righteous cause. His enemies might wreak vengeance on his child. What better hiding-place for the babe than this yeoman's house ? And was there not a precedent in the story of the Shepherd Earl, Lord of Skipton, who had been reared on a Cumbrian farm to conceal him from his adversaries ?

The lady of high degree, before she left her wicker basket and its contents in the porch, had made enquiries stealthily, no doubt, and knew all about Mistress Dean's hunger for a girl-child and the soft, brave heart the yeoman carried ; and the only ruthless thing about the affair was the agony of her own mother-love when the time came for going out alone from the farmstead's porch. Or, again, the child might have been left motherless, and the father, pursued and all but spent, have given some trusty henchman orders to find a home for the child he could not take with him. There is no end to beguiling speculation ; and often as I pass the farm outside my gate, the question comes, " Whose was the babe in the wicker basket ? " The novelist would tell you in the last chapter. You would know all about it—the mystery ended, and you the poorer because your fancy could play no more about its dear intricacies.

Almost under my feet, where I sit here with Linton's yesterdays, there is another mystery still unsolved. Over and over again I have been tempted to pry into it; yet it remains a question, instinct with romance. This part of the house is certainly as old as the days when Fountains Abbey possessed most of the lands from here to the high fells bordering Malham. The Abbey owned my own house, too, and knowledge of the fact suggests one solution of the mystery.

A corner of my room is wider than the room below, and the space underneath is unaccounted for. Whatever measurements one takes, one comes back always to the certainty that a chamber six feet square and eight feet or so in height lies hidden. No human eyes have seen it, maybe, since it was used as a priest's hiding-place after Fountains and its kindred Abbeys were turned to other uses, and those of the Old Faith were a hunted people.

There is as small a " priest's hiding-hole " as this at Lawkland Hall, within the sanctuary of its private chapel. A few rough steps lead down to it. The priest might have been celebrating Mass at peril of the rack—might have been surprised by clamour of a knocking at the very door—and have disappeared as completely as if the earth had swallowed him. As indeed it had, for one breathless moment of escape, as he heard the discomfited pursuers go out, snarling because the prey had " gone away " just when they seemed sure of him.

Is that what lies below me—a place left to its silence and its memories since the last priest was surprised at Mass and sought refuge in its narrow compass ? Or does this chamber hide stark and utter tragedy ? All that is left of some luckless fellow may wait to bring silent witness to some foul deed long since hidden out of sight. Yet I know, somehow, that no bones lie there among the musty raiment that once clothed their flesh.

There's a quiet, friendly haunting round about the house. One sees nothing, hears nothing, except now and then the swish of silken robes about the corridors and stairs; but, when one comes home tired or out of heart, a fragrance as of lavender steals through the hall, and *Somebody* is close at hand with restful sympathy. We of the house long since learned to name our guardian lady, *Somebody*, a name given in sheer affection. She is from far-off times, I think. Why she should choose to stay on, when passed for promotion to a finer world, one does not know ; but we are the gainers.

An ancient stone stands upright on the hill beyond the garden here. Anyone familiar with the " gathering stones " of Northumberland at once declares it a rallying place for the manhood of the parish when invasion threatened. It may well have been. We were a long stride further from the Border than Northumberland, but the range of the same invaders took Linton in its course.

There is a persistent legend in the village that the stone, whatever its earlier purposes, was used to light Threshfield folk over from the far side of the hill to service at White Abbey here, when winter's nights were dark. There is no lettering of any sort upon the stone, no mark save of the weather's tooth ; but set deep in lead on its top is an iron socket, such as was used in older days to hold a cresset. It needs small imagination to picture the same monk who lit the cresset to guide the Threshfield faithful to evensong, lighting it afresh on some stark midwinter night, after the messenger had galloped from the north with tidings of a new Scots raid. Lathered with sweat and spume, they came, he and his horse, and halted in their stride.

" Light the cresset ! The Scots will be pouring down at daybreak."

He was gone with that. And the monk sped up to the hilltop ; and when the Linton stalwarts gathered with quick answer, and those of Threshfield trooped over to the summons, the man of peace blessed them as they went north to meet the enemy.

He who first gave me the legend of the stone was in straight descent from Christopher Dean, who constabled the township and found a wicker basket in his porch; and, when he went from us, a great gap seemed to open in the Dale, as if his narrow grave-space widened to the further hills that would know his step no more. Charitable, wise, quick when at rare times need asked him to show a mettled temper, he lived finely in the present because his race, like Wharfe River, knew the far streamlets of its past. About him always there was the free air of the higher fells, the sun and sleet and circumstance that his ancestors had shared. There are so many questions I want to ask him now he's gone. He knew, not only Linton's history and the tale of every acre bordering it, but the Dale's wider story, past and present. To be in doubt on any point was to know where to go for a true counsellor.

The village is very quiet as I sit here, letting long thoughts roam out, and thinking of what such men as this dead yeoman, bred of yeomen, mean to the fabric of our country life. No pipe we ever smoked together failed to bring some tale—racy, or sad, or gay—curling up into the twisted clouds of our own making. And now, as I linger with memory of him, it seems that in all our little " township " only the owls and myself are awake and busy. They are hawking game for their larder. So am I—for the larder of a spirit hungering for the things that were.

As if in answer to one's need, a faint music tinkles down the Skipton Road, and ripens into the beat of hoofs—*tink-tink*, *tinkety-trot-and-tink*—and a voice roars out through the night, " Oh, take the reins and be durned to you! You know the road by this time."

It is " Sandy," as we will name him, returning as of yore from Skipton Market—Sandy, who persists in the faith that horseflesh is good enough for him, whoever else chooses to gad about in a tin box. They say there are few yards of the highway-wall that Sandy has not collided with, through the years of market-daying out from Skipton. Yet he survives at seventy, with the sound common-sense of old to leave it to his nag at such times. They always reach the home-gate—farmer and gig and horse—and Sandy, for the remainder of the week, is a shrewd, keen husbandman, knowing how to get the best from his lands and the men who till them.

Sandy should have been killed long since on the Skipton Road, or have died in his bed of heart failure. He persists in doing neither, and the lessening clamour of his gig, as it goes up-Dale, is a lusty home song to me. He and I have " summered and wintered each other," as the saying goes, and many better-seeming men are windlestraws, set side by side with him. As long as Sandy lasts, there's a hard-bitten Dalesman left among us still. And, when he goes, he will return to haunt the Skipton Road.

XIII

MEMORIES

The Dancing Parson—" Hipping-Stones "—A Crucifix—" Witch Stones "—The Skipton Road.

I DOUBT if any village, south or north, has Linton's many-sided interest, packed into such little compass. Never a modern house intrudes into its comeliness. It is the home of people who from of old have led free lives, untouched by the herd-instinct that levels individuality. Its parsons, no less than their flocks, claimed the right to follow their bent, and earned reputations for oddity. One of these—a nephew of Sir Isaac Newton—had a consuming hobby for dancing. He would take the trouble to cross to Paris, in days when the journey was arduous, to learn fresh steps, and return to Linton Rectory with new-fed zeal.

The pastime—curious enough in itself—was rendered odder still by his aloofness from all fellow-dancers, though Linton was noted for the light feet of its men and women when they took the floor. He had a man-servant at the Rectory who was skilled at the fiddle. The master, in his best wearing-gear, would dance in front of a great mirror, admiring the rhythm of his paces. The servant was pledged to fiddle with his back turned to the dancer, and on forfeit of his life not to turn his head. Once the fiddler did turn for a curious glance. The parson saw him in the mirror; and murder was nearly done in earnest.

" I just ran," the man explained later on to cronies in the village inn—"ran as if the Devil himself was after me. And parson's a sweet-tempered man at usual times."

The very ordering of the parish was unusual in those days. Like Burnsall, a few miles lower down the Dale, it had two Rectors—and two Rectories, facing each other across their separate gardens. Each house, they say, had its "squint-window," from which each incumbent could look privily on what his neighbour did. The Rectors took alternate services in Linton Church—Matins one week, Evensong the next—and it must have made for an astounding muddlement. Suppose one was Puritan, the other a King's man, in the days of civil strife—what hope was there for the village folk? They would be going two ways all the time. For sermons counted in those days.

The Rectors came through it all, somehow, keeping their true selves true. The one that makes insistent appeal, to my own fancy, is he who forgot to take his written sermon with him to Linton Church, and got up into the pulpit, and smiled at large upon his people.

"By good luck I've forgotten my sermon," said he, "and I'll give you a chapter out of the Old Testament that's worth twenty of it. Ay, and I'll put wrath and judgment right between the middle of your ribs, like east wind from over Simon's Seat."

Candid and thorough, that old-time parson. And they tackled the east wind in their ribs, doubtless, as they took fairer weather—all in the day's work, and the best at the core of both to be gathered, Dalesman-wise, for further betterment.

Another parson, living in one's own house here, was responsible for the stepping-stones—"hipping-stones," in native speech—that run from the stream-gate of the garden to Well Lane. His only eccentricity was a love of solitude, and by bridging the stream in this way he was able to get out into the fields without covering a yard of village highroad. One is grateful to him. Rugged or graceful, bridges have their own compelling charm; but romance of a deep and tender sort goes always with the hipping-stones. They do not rear themselves high, disdainful of the waters they have conquered. They chat with the stream, making little melodies and roundelays of its impatience to get through the barriers. Neither are they insistent to claim victory always ; for there are times when floods break down from the moor, and no man can see the stones at all, or cross by them. A give-and-take life they spend together, the stones and the river, friends in spite of rivalry, or because of it.

The staidest folk, somehow, cannot help busying themselves with romance when they linger beside such a stream as Linton's, spanned by mossy stones. They grow curiously impatient if, at the least, a village beauty is not crossing at the moment, her ankles slim and timorous above the flood. Their full expecta-tion is to see her swain leaping from the further brink to guide her over. No village, of course, can provide these pleasing things at call ; but always there's the hope of them.

If it is true that every house is haunted where men have lived and died, it is just as true of the lanes their feet have trodden, the meadows where they swung the scythe in rhythmic answer to the lark's high joy in sunlight and the thrift of life—true of the dark tracks they followed when storm-witches rode out from the north-east, pushing their kindred sleet in front of them with brooms as big as the mountains.

The acres just beyond my house are surely haunted. They are full of baffling, half-guessed lore. Where the garden slips out into the pasture bordering the stream, all is usual. The dipper whose mate is sitting on her nest under the sycamore roots that hollow down to the water, is glancing forward and back between the two water-gates that mark his right of way. His white breast shows against the sable as he stands on a boulder curtseying. Then he's into the water, wading along its bed in search of food for the bright-eyed mate who awaits his coming.

A kingfisher arrives—swift, like a glimpse of some blue heaven denied to all but him—a glory and a miracle. A heron follows, wide sailing on grey pinions. And everywhere the lambs are running races, heedless of the mother-ewes that bleat, in frantic, silly woe.

All is new. It is the year's spring in this sheltered hollow; but on the hill-top, where the pillar stands that once held a cresset to light the Threshfield folk, all is old on the sudden.

Where the garden slips out into the pasture

The shape of the rounded hill, the sweep of greensward on the further side, the great boulders, set in ordered array by men of some far-off age, suggest insistently that here was once a British encampment. The boulders are no haphazard outcrop of the limestone, one here, another there. They stand close together, curving to the sweep of what must have been a wide half-circle; and below them is a strip of woodland, sloping sheer to stream-level, up which an enemy might be expected to move cunningly to the assault.

Tradition gives no news of what the place was in the misty days when warriors painted their bodies with woad and wielded uncouth fighting tools. Skilled antiquaries have taken bearings here and have unveiled something of the past. It seems certain that a camp of no mean importance stood on this site where lambs gambol on the daisied turf. So once more, going further back in time, one has to reconstruct the full meaning of that upright stone on the hill. In its young days, apparently, it was the centre of any final rally that might be forced on hard-pressed Britons. It has yet another use to-day, and a farm-lad assured me once that the pillar was set there as a rubbing-post for cattle. For proof absolute he pointed to it.

"Seeing's believing," said he. "There's our old skew-horned Jenny rubbing herself at it this very minute."

Standing on the hill this blithe spring morning, one is astonished afresh by the wonder of this pasture-field. A well-known face is always harder to describe than a new one, met at some eager turning of the road. The intimacies of long affection, the joyous and troubled moods shared with this corner of the world—growth, and decay, and lusty growth again that one has watched beside its stream and primrosed hollows—they are loved so well that it is difficult to praise.

Village-ward, Linton's homesteads lie billowed in a foam of leafage. Sycamore and chestnut, rowan and elm and white-beam, are unfronding slender laceries that let the blue sky through. The stream runs silver-grey between islets of gold kingcups, and the sleepy land below is stirred by ceaseless babel of over-wheeling rooks. Turn westward, and Threshfield's grey, friendly houses glance at you from under their own flood of leafing trees. Over it all stand the high fells and the higher moors, guardians and lovers of what to them are "the children lands at play." A whole winter was worth battling with, to earn the roomy joy of one such day as this.

Yet soon the past is reaching upward from the soil again. You cannot escape it anywhere about these old acres bordering Linton. Not many years since men were rebuilding a barn at the far end of the village, and out of the dust and litter a queer, soiled piece of metal emerged. They rubbed it bright, and the owner of the barn—another son of Christopher Dean, yeoman and Parish Constable—knew it for what it was, a Crucifix of brass. The very crudeness of its workmanship was proof of the simple piety that had fashioned it. It went to the British Museum for advice as to its date; and they, coveting

Linton's homesteads lie billowed in a foam of leafage

it, named a price. It was of Norman workmanship, it seemed, and vastly rare. Christopher Dean's son had another view of the matter. He could not understand that price, in terms of money, could remotely touch what was his by right of finding. It rests now on a pillar of old Linton Kirk, looking down on the place where the Deans worshipped when Elizabeth was Queen of England, and Mary o' Scots roamed from one dread prison to the next.

The finding of the treasure-trove brought me in contact with one of those singular, fresh-visioned wanderers who seem to be my luck in life. Silver-haired, with youth in his step and merry eyes, he came to ask where the relic was to be seen. When I told him, he smiled with quaint, wayward humour.

"A very suitable resting-place," he said. "You may know that in the dark, superstitious Middle Ages, it was the farmers' custom to put Crucifixes in barns, for blessing of the cattle. In our enlightened times, they put stones with a hole in them, to scare away the witches."

His point neatly made, he saluted me with old-world courtesy and went down the road, out of reach for ever to all but memory. He was a true observer of the Dale. These "witch stones," to be found still above the headstalls of a byre, date back to a remote and widespread superstition. They are small. Their magic is of no avail unless they have been taken from the stream that bored the little hole in them. And yet their other name of "self-bored stones" seems to deny the water's agency.

One cannot unravel the intertwining skeins of superstition's lore. Across the water from my garden is a walled, ruined corner, green with moss and ferns, where hounds were kept once in the olden days. The huntsman lived just beyond in the house, now a place of mystery and twilit charm, where a joiner plies his craft amid the nameless fragrance made up of old tree-trunks and new sawdust, glue and beeswax. The shutters, once barred and closed at night, lie always open now, and painted in what once was white stands a circle with a square inside it. The huntsman when he pulled his shutters to, drew in the painted token; and it too, was a charm to scare away the witches, though few are left among us to remember such old whys and wherefores. It is also a tramp "sign," when scrawled on a gate in chalk, and means that the owner of the house is "pious, but tidy for a trifle."

Why should the tramps, a people ancient as the gypsies and the tinkers and the besom-makers, have chosen the exact symbol that has power against the witches? I do not know. But, as regards the tramping sort, I have my own useful knowledge, and my own piece of chalk. When they gather in battalions, not by single spies, I chalk a simple square on my own gate. It means that the master keeps a hefty dog, and has a heart of granite.

The mind, once allowed to roam in a homeland it knows by heart, is hard to check. One memory suggests another, in endless sequence, like cloud and sunlight playing hide-and-seek on the abiding hills. To think of Linton Bridge—the big one of the three—is to recall without warning a quaint adventure that befell two travellers.

There was no big bridge then, and all horsed traffic went through the ford. Tom Airey of Girston drove the mail-cart in and out of Skipton, and one dark night—the mist hiding all but a yard in front of his lamps—he came to the ford with his two passengers. The stream was in spate, as it happened, and the strangers, thinking he had mistaken his way, leapt out in panic search for safety. They found themselves in a deep swirl of waters, clutched at the mail-cart frantically, and were dragged up again somehow by a driver who had also to attend to his scared horses. All that he said, when they settled to the road again, was brief and like himself.

"You're wetter than you need be, friends. It comes of not trusting Tom Airey to know the Skipton Road."

And with that memory old thoughts come flooding back. The Skipton Road—it means so much to its devotees. Romance and history stride mile by mile with it. Rylstone, planted like a garden with free-blooming flowers of memory, nestles in its hollow of comely houses and wide-branched trees; the toll-bar, quiet now, but once the scene of elopements and ambushes and wild uproar when the nights were dark; None-go-by, where once her left shoe was claimed from every bride who passed that way, by some right whose origin was lost long since in the mists of yester-year; the raking fells and forest-lands, where deer roamed up to the elder lands of Hubberholme and

Oughtershaw—what can any lover make of it all but a song that lilts along the Skipton Road?

Nowhere on those good miles will you find cloying prettiness. Hollies and thorn-trees and tough-rooted alders are its shrubs. Sweet of the wild-rose blossom, strong fragrance of the honey-suckle and bird-cherry—they've earned their right to holiday, as the pastures and lush meadows have, by sturdy fighting through a winter quick to come and slow to go. From moor to tinkling valley-stream, this spendthrift glory of the summer is a thing hard-won and real. If one has shared the road's winters and its sleet-driven nights, it talks in the days of its prosperity with a voice incredibly sufficing.

Humour is abroad, too, along its twisting miles. There's a wooden fence nowadays on the left hand of the road as you go to Skipton. Below it is a steep bank, falling to a broad strip of ditchland, once unguarded, whose story goes back to the time when Miss Blake, of happy Rylstone memory, was alive among us—a great lady, friend of all the Dale. Lady Anne Clifford, I think, set this fashion of big-hearted gentlewomen who thread generation after generation of our story with their quiet, insistent presence. We have them to-day among us. Miss Blake had been driven by Richard, her gardener-coachman, to a ball, and on the return journey he, or his horses, missed the road, and they all fell into the bottom of the ditch, filled with melting snow. There was a time of confusion, and then the mistress, disentangling herself, stood in a foot of ice-cold water.

"When you're *quite* ready, Richard, we'll proceed," she said, with dignity.

The Skipton Road. Weather and traffic along it—dawns one has seen redden over its fells—gloamings rosy-soft as dreams—horsemen and drovers and market folk giving a cheery "all's well with the world"—these are woof and weft of its glamour still. Nothing can rob one of the spirit of old that comes as one rides home from Skipton in the lush murk of twilight and sees the lamplight stream out across the highway from Linton Hall. "*Stryke, Daykin, the devil's in the hemp*"—the legend takes shape and substance as you pass, a strong happening, not to be denied, that still lives on. The village lights give the next welcome of to-day. You know those who live inside these lamp-lit houses, and they know you. You've summered and wintered each other, according to the good, oft-repeated phrase. Sometimes they've helped you in need, and sometimes it was the other way. All is forgotten of how and why, except the quiet neighbourliness that beats at the village heart. A farm-dog barks as you pass. The owls give their hunting-cry. The rooks send up a sleepy, fretful cawing. And afterwards the high fells send their sleep among us—a thrifty and a tranquil slumber, bred of great content.

XIV

" LILE EMILY'S " BRIDGE

The Old Trout—A Truthful Voice—Pam the Fiddler—Quarry Hollow—" Jannock "—Dale's Names.

OF all Dale's words, perhaps "lile" is the subtlest and most tender. It means "little," but with a difference. Man, woman, or child can be plain little, but few are spoken of as "lile." Affection of old standing—admiration, guarded, but fast of root—a whole world of feeling goes to it. They give that title to the crooked, slender bridge in the hollow and to Emily Norton, who crossed by it to sanctuary of the miller's house.

As you go from Linton to the foot of Greet Bank, you come to a corner of the Dale remote from nowadays. It is a hamlet in itself, sheltered from wind and tempest ; and it is peopled thick with memories. The Linton and the Threshfield becks, mated and content, flow under coppice trees. Emily's bridge crosses this stream to the silent water-mill that once ground corn for all the parish ; and I was standing there, one moist summer's evening, intent on watching the pool that lay under shadow of the low parapet. Christopher Dean's son chanced to come by at the moment, and eyed me with good-humoured raillery.

" Wishing you had a rod in your hand ? " he asked, divining my inmost heart. " Well, it would be no manner of use. Jacky the trout was there in my father's days—and in Noah's, they do say. We've all had a go at him in our time."

I admitted as much, recalling more than one adventure when I had nearly brought him to bank—always nearly.

" He's too old and wise for us," my neighbour went on. " Jacky has studied a lot, down there in his pool—ay, and laughed a goodish bit, I fancy. And nobody knows what he weighs."

" Dan o' the Heights does. He hooked him once, and played him for five hours, up and down between Bow Bridge and this, and got his landing net under him at last."

We all know Dan, and Christopher Dean's son chuckled quietly.

" Ay, and the net broke under Jacky's weight. According to Dan, he was something between a shark and a littlish whale."

It was then, as we idled together in the long-drawn gloaming, that for the first time my neighbour unloosed his tongue about the story of this bridge on which we stood.

" Some say—and folk will say aught—that Jacky was an old trout when lile Emily Norton crossed here. There'd been trouble in the Rylstone country, and the miller sheltered her till it went by."

" What trouble ? " I asked, a sleuth-hound on the trail of legend.

" It had to do with some sort of a Catholic Rising, longer ago than I know aught about. Old Norton was for it, and all his sons ; and they lost. That's how the Deans have had the tale, generations out of mind."

Here was a voice at my elbow, a truthful voice. Historians always romance, on one side or another of their tale—not consciously, but following their inborn prejudices. Legend, of the yeoman's kind, has no bias either way. It tells simply what has been simply told by fore-elders, and lets it stand at that.

" Tell me more of Lile Emily," I prompted.

He is shy for awhile, as the old trout under the bridge distrusts all eager lures. Then I tempt him to the bank again.

"Her men were scattered—all except Deerfoot, nimble once on his feet, but too old for the wars. So it was he that brought lile Emily to the brigg here, and into the miller's caring."

I have gleaned knowledge of one episode in the ill-fated Rising of the North unknown to history as such. Froude himself—who has kept alive for us the record of Christopher Aske's fine deed in Skipton—would have revelled in this

" Lile Emily's " bridge

narrative, quiet and sure in detail, that is given me to-night because the hour and the place have drawn memories from a neighbour of long, ripe ancestry. Such men as Procter Dean are torch-bearers, surely, lighting the gallant past grown dim to modern vision.

Dusk steals upward from the water, not down from the sky that is still rose-pink and daffodil and tenderest blue. More and more this corner of our little world shows like a hamlet, secure within its ordered boundaries. A cluster of barns and cottages slopes up the darkening fields. A homely lamp-glow shows at a window. The stream's tinkle-tankle, the big-bosomed song of Wharfe River close at hand, are music of an elder day. Of an elder day, too, is the school, just beyond, where our farm lads and lasses are taught arithmetic and what not. They are taught more than ever they guess, one fancies, by ancient voices lingering still about the schoolhouse.

A more homely building than Burnsall's faultless school, its atmosphere is no whit less Elizabethan ; and strange tales linger round its walls and ample playground. One schoolmaster of bygone times, known as Pam the Fiddler, has given a legend to the wooded highway-corner that makes folk of an older generation hurry by o' nights. Pam's fiddle was his second self. Out of school hours he carried it with him up the moorland glens, and played the very elves from their hiding-holes between the tree roots. On winter's evenings, when his flock had scampered home from work and he was left to pile fuel higher on a lonely fire, Pam drew strange music from his fiddle—tripping airs, fit for nimble feet to dance to, and wild laments, and Puck-like, impish tunes.

Then by-and-by his fame was noised abroad, and they would not let him fiddle for the solace of his own private soul. They tempted him to play at country fairs and weddings, where the ale ran strong. And by-and-by the Rector of the parish—a grim and austere man—came down to the school, and found Pam fiddling in the playground by the light of a young, sickle moon. Pam drew such threads of magic across the strings that they woke and throbbed, as a maid's heart throbs when her chosen, from out of the world of men, takes her lips and claims them.

The Rector snatched Pam's fiddle from his hands, and spat a sermon at him. And the two men closed in bitter strife. Pam, little and lithe, fought desperately against his bulky parish priest ; but in the last result he crumpled up, and lay there, still and quiet. The parson, once he was sure of the sorry end to his sermon, stole out for spade and pick-axe, and buried Pam, with the sickle moon looking on between a scudding rack of cloud. It had been a fair fight, and he had never meant to kill his man.

So he said a prayer above the corpse and the grave of his own making, and went his ways. And soon afterwards the hardiest men whose business took them past the school at dusk were apt to hear a strange and eerie fiddling round about the playground when the children's laughter and their feet had ceased to make its day-time music. We hear it still, some of us who come home when dusk leans down to night-time. Traffic may be busy on the road by day; but the fret of its journeys ceases now. Pam and his fiddle are alive among us once again—these, and the night-jar's eerie note.

A legend older by far still persists among the village folk. They seldom speak of it, and then only with a disarming smile at its absurdity. They are far from knowing that they perpetuate the Pan myth. Pan, and Pam the Fiddler, are mixed inextricably in this ancient version of the tale. They tell you that on certain nights, when the school fire has died into grey embers, an unearthly glow fills the room, so that no passer-by can fail to see it. They tell of "old Pam," with a goat's bearded head protruding above the decent clothes of a schoolmaster. And about him are eleven little scholars, all with goats' heads, listening as he teaches them the Rule of Three and thwacks their hairy sides when wits are dull.

It is an ancient corner of the Dale, and a haunted. From the school a lean pasture climbs to the Threshfield highway, where the little quarry is. They took stones and gravel from it once, to mend the roads; but they began to undermine roots of spreading sycamores and beeches that make a glory of the highway corner, and we care greatly for our trees. So the little quarry is left nowadays to its dreams. It is a special haunt of nesting birds and wildflowers and children. One tree alone, with its gnarled and hollow trunk, is a cave of old romance for any healthy-minded bairn who is intent on knights and dragons. Mosses carpet the boulder-stones with a richness all their own. Anenomes, frail as the breeze that stirs them, push up in spring, when the spiked " lords and ladies " have blossomed and gone by. The place is singular in its beauty, its sense of remoteness from the highway that carries traffic just beyond its guardian wall. It is singular, too, by reason of a haunting known to many whose journeys take them past it when dusk and its silences begin to speak.

Norton Tower

None has seen or heard anything to make for terror. Yet out of the quarry comes a stealthy, inexplicable dread that quickens heart and feet. Many have felt its spell; and they laugh at it in daylight hours, without conviction. A few years since they found a man's skeleton while they were quarrying for gravel. The haunting seemed explained, till they had a " Crowner's Quest " on the bones, and old folk of the parish witnessed to the fact that a gypsy had been taken ill while his people camped in the hollow. Probably he had died there. It was common knowledge that gypsies hated the delays attendant upon legal burial, and foul play need have no connection with hasty interment in a wood. When one of theirs died, they dug the readiest grave for him, and passed on next day with the caravans that did not like their wheels to rust. So that explanation of the haunting does not serve. Long and long ago, one fancies, some drear happening drenched this hollow with slaughter and the cries of stricken men.

In the field that slopes from this quarry to the Elizabethan schoolhouse, between one scud of thunder-rain and the next, I encountered something talked of by the elders as a rare sight, happening once or twice in a lifetime. An earth-rainbow, they named it ; and that describes it with quiet precision. This sort of rainbow does not arch the sky, tempting the superstitious to search for fairy-gold where it dips to ground. It has neither beginning nor end, but floods every crumpled hollow of the pastures with an ever-moving restlessness of colour—crimsons and blues, rich golden yellows, purples that cream in royal glory up to the fields' high tops. None, having seen it once, can forget the glamour of this far-strewn pageant.

One diverting story of the haunting round about the Elizabethan school came to me from a neighbour who "had just returned from a burying." Men grow reminiscent at these times. He told me how, as a boy, he was a scholar at the school, in William Harker's time there as dominie. The big crab-apple tree at the far side of the playground was ripe with fruit.

" Me and Dick Metcalfe came down one night, and climbed the tree, and filled our pockets. And after that we ran a race."

" What sort of race ? "

" Well, we'd crossed no further than a yard o' the school-yard before a terrible big roaring sounded. It was moonlight, you understand ; and there, right in t' middle o' the yard, was a hairy sort o' monster, wearing our schoolmaster's clothes. And he opened his jaws at us."

He lights his pipe afresh, with the true narrator's art, before proceeding.

" We ran, Dick Metcalfe and me. Begow, we ran, till neither

foot knew which was hindmost! Both were i' front, I fancy, at one and the same time. And we never stopped till our bellows needed mending at the top of Girston Hill. 'It was Barguest, right enough,' says Dick Metcalfe. 'You're a fool,' says I. 'It was Old Pam himself.' So with that we got to fighting. I earned a black eye, and Dick's nose was bigger than it need be, and we cleared up our fright that way. But to this day I go pratly when I pass yond old school corner."

Pratly! The old Dalesmen would be a delight if only for this gift of dropping a time-tried word that survives because it expresses what no other could. To go pratly is to walk as silently as may be, with circumspection and fear at the back of one's heart—as Agag walked, one fancies. The next moment my companion wanders from memories of the crab-tree and Old Pam to a yeoman who had died at eighty further up the Dale.

"I rode out to view the corpse, as a friend should, and the widow was dropping tears on her Bible as she turned from page to page. 'It's a great loss, to be sure,' says I, clumsy at comforting women. 'Well,' says she, 'it didn't stand to reason he could live much longer. What's worriting me is finding a text for his tombstone later on.' 'Don't you be worriting,' says I. ' " *He died as he lived—jannock.*" That's what all the Dale thinks o' Tant Wiseman, and that's what you'll have carved on his stone.' And with that she puts her apron to her eyes. And, 'Thank ye, John,' says she. 'I'd never have thought o' that.' And then she went about the burial meats, brisk as a bee in summer."

My wayfarer has gone, into the stillness of a fragrant night. A farm-dog challenges his tread. And I stay on, thinking of that good word "jannock." It implies fair-dealing, and the little more that means so much. A man once given the name has the freedom of the Dale conferred on him; and if he chanced to be left derelict, by fault of bad seasons or bankrupt debtors, Dalesmen would trust him to the end of time.

Thoughts chase each other in a tranquil riot, here in this folded hollow of the moors. What's in a name ? Everything that matters, one is tempted to think at times. Names are the nurseries of deeds. From Skipton out to Oughtershaw there was a fashion once to baptize the eldest-born " Christopher." History knows what a gallant pair was reared to manhood on that name —Christopher Aske, of Skipton, who saved the honour of softly-nurtured women from the rabble—Kit Norton, who rescued Mary o' Scots from prison, the only one among her devotees to do what many planned. Froude, the wizard who touched history with a painter's living brush, was stirred by these two exploits to vivid prose.

In the Dale are other Christophers, strong at tillage and sheep-saving up the winter heights, of whom the world outside hears nothing. Yet their lives seem to be instinct with all their birth-name stands for—strength, and a fine simplicity.

Rich in pastures striding to the high moors and the sky, rich in moorlands that send out their heather-crimson, beacons lit to brother beacons when August comes, rich in watered ghylls and woodlands where spring leaps out in sudden foam of leafage, the Dale has great wealth, too, in the names it has given to its fields and hills and valleys. Lauradale—a field bordering the village here—has a melody about it that suggests lilac-time and maids in sprigged muslin and June in its careless flood. Lauradale. Once it has sung itself into your mind, you never get away from the soft, persuasive lilt. And what of Bridle-Stiles, the twisting pack-horse track that goes, forgotten now, between its limestone walls ? The name sings in its own way, and will not be denied. Leaving the hill-road from Cracoe out to Thorpe, it winds down until it loses itself among the pastures ; but once it was the route to Girston, and forded Wharfe below Linton's grey and comely church.

What, too, of Farlands Coppice? Fancy spins romance about the name. It sets the heart tingling for adventure and such stuff as midsummer nights are made of. Anything but the sordid prose of things could live in such a place—dreams that survive the waking, and shapes of beauty dancing on light feet. It is a woodland, surely, where all the butterflies are blue.

These places with beguiling names are close at hand ; but Linton has no monopoly of them. To those who know the names of field and hill, as a man knows his children's, the Dale has a music threading all its way. Some are stern as their gaunt, rocky screes. Some are frolicsome and tender. Now and then you come to a field with a name that baffles understanding. "Goindra" is one of them. It, too, has a queer music of its own. Alone among all our field names, it has suffered from no explanations. The hardiest of explorers in this lore has never, to my knowledge, ventured a surmise as to what Goindra means, or to what tongue the name belongs.

As you go past Kilnsey and up through the grey lands to Arncliffe—redshanks and plover busy all the way, if you take the road in spring—you are in Amerdale. And how should that sing to a man, except with joy that a name so happy could have been coined by alchemy of ancient folk-speech? . You go up Amerdale, past Arncliffe's ordered and surprising beauty. Great bluffs of limestone rear themselves to the sky above the green, quiet lowlands. The track winds up, grey in its scuds of sunlit dust. And now you are in Langstrothdale Chase. The Cliffords hunted deer from Skipton, right up through this wild Chase, with the name that rings like hoof-beats. Sturdy riders on mettlesome nags—a great-hearted stag in front—stride of the ceaseless gallop and cream of the lathered flanks—men had the gift of speech when the word Langstrothdale was born.

Peny-Ghent looks down on Langstrothdale. It is a mountain grim and sheer against the sky, and no one seems to know what its name is doing here in northern fastnesses. Cornish or Welsh it might be; but it is foreign to our northern ears, and puzzles us. Yet it *strides*, as all names do in this free land of stream and rock, of birds that sit like sable clouds in the sky, hunting their prey. What's in a name? More than folk understand. Once—long ago, as time is counted in these hurrying days—a carrier's cart went up and down the dale. On its board was painted " Amorous Stanley." He was a good carrier, civil and punctilious, but he lived up to the name that had been given him at birth with light-hearted unconcern.

Names, somehow, are prayers for the future. And that is why one longs that the Dale should return to the old habit of naming its sons Christopher.

XV

THRESHFIELD

The Besom-Maker—Uncle Robert—The Rose's Call.

THE field-track from Linton wanders "crazy-ways" till
it saunters downward to a stile beneath high trees;
and suddenly the grey highroad meets one, dipping to
Threshfield Bridge and climbing afterwards into the village.

Rich as the Dale is in its bridges, Threshfield's holds its own
among them all. Its beauty of line, massive yet simple, borrows
greater charm from its clustered farm-buildings, from the stream
that goes broad and lazy underneath its arches. Higher up, the
beck has an eager, hurried life, like most of our upland water-
ways; but here it stays to dream. When March has almost
done its worst and soft airs begin to roam abroad, great spikes of
water-dock look down at their crimson shadows in the pools.
Then the marsh marigolds are gay from bank to bank, gold as the
heart of summer. And afterwards the brown-yellow musk
flowers throw their pride of bloom across the drowsy brook.

It is a corner that might have been stolen from Thomas
Hardy's country, or from some delectable hamlet of Sussex,
bordering Rye and Winchelsea. The farm-cart, deep in the
water to swell its shrunken axles—the logs waiting to be sawn
for hearth-wood—the thrifty smell of byre and stable—all are
of the spacious days, when toil knew no hurry and men slept
sound o' nights.

The Besom-Maker lived in the comfortable, quiet house

beside the stream. He was born under its roof, and had learned all that eighty years and odd could teach him of love for the old homestead—and for the Dale. There are new brooms nowadays, machine-made. They do not sweep as clean as Threshfield's. That is common knowledge, for its trade survives all competition of new-fangled besoms.

I met him once half-way up the road to Threshfield Moor, as he was coming down with a great load of heather on his shoulders. The lean, wiry figure, stooping under its burden, the background of swart heath and sunlit sky, asked for a painter's brush. Such clear-cut pictures come to one every now and then, interpreting the meaning and romance of a man's trade.

" It's warmish," said the Besom-Maker, setting down his load.

The suggestion that he had chosen a warmish time of day for the job was met by the rejoinder that life was full of compensations. The sun was hot ; but then his burden shielded his head. Moreover, he explained, it was good to be alive, and he'd never been one to blame the sun for shining. Men saw far too little of him in these latter years.

So we had got round to the weather, as Dalesmen must. I put it to him that the seasons had changed utterly, though it was the fashion to say that they had been always as we know them nowadays.

" Changed ? Why, we've no seasons. Time was when winter had a keen tooth of its own, and set about its business properly. It finished with March, and April saw cattle grazing in the pastures. Farmers are lucky now if their beasts are out o' byre in May."

From that we drifted into talk of besom-making, and the face of this ancient man was a joy to watch. Its wrinkles, hard-earned and deep, smiled happily. The brave old eyes grew bright. With so little said, one captured somehow the under-music that informed his craftsmanship; and that is why, I take it, his brooms had such a hefty swish with them.

All that goes to the making of a besom he gathered in the open—tough heather stems from the moor, handles from the hazel thickets. The very " tying-bands " of bark were shredded by himself, and the tools he used, of a strong and fine simplicity, were handed down to him by forbears skilled in the using.

A great lover of horses, he. Horse and pony shoes are clustered over his stable-door, not only for luck, but for remembrance of dead favourites. Now his time has come to take the further journey, surely he has found heather on the moor, and hazel thickets pranked with primroses in spring, and the horses he has lost in this life.

He died at a time of snow, and his last wish was gratified. They buried him at his wife's side, high up on Greenhow Hill, where the little graveyard lies open to every wind that blows. There is a strong, abiding picture in one's mind of that day, too— as of the morning when one met him crowned with heather for his besoms as he came down from Threshfield Moor.

Greenhow was white and desolate, stretching across a wilderness untamed, untameable. The fences guarding ancient lead-mines straggled black among deep snows. All was austerity and silence till a little breeze got up, eager and unafraid. It was the requiem of one who had never feared heat o' the sun or roke of the wintry tops.

Over the bridge, and topping the gentle rise, Threshfield's ancient peace abides. The house with the rose-window has many a story locked away within its walls, if it would tell them. The cottages, roomy and old, are proud of their wayside gardens, disdaining the dust of passing traffic.

One cannot think of Threshfield village without " Uncle Robert." He, too, has left us; but he only seemed to go. His heart was too wedded to the village, like the Besom-

Maker's, his personality too strong, for such a cold and long farewell.

He is with us still, this big, tough Dalesman who died game at eighty. Sometimes, as you pass the door of his one-time tavern, "The Old Hall Inn," you almost see him standing there, big and lusty, a host of the elder breed. When they're mowing

Threshfield's ancient peace

the great meadow down by Threshfield Beck, you seem to hear his voice, chiding the laggards, cheering the hefty, while the sweat drips from him as he works among the labourers.

There are times also when, crossing the high pastures, you're aware of a rider, big on a striding horse, who counts the tally of his lambs along the uplands. That, too, is Uncle Robert, home again with mixed weather at the birth-time of the farming year.

In all things he was singularly alive. His ready wit could hold its own against most comers. No shams or "play-acting" ever passed the barrier of his quick, sane judgment; and his way with such was truculent, a delight to honest onlookers. His knowledge of horses and dogs, crops and weather and human nature, was profound. Yet the quality that stands out in clearest shape—clearer with every year that passes—was his fine tenacity. He chose his road and stuck to it, whatever hazard came.

Tenacity. That one word recurs to mind, over and over again, like the rat-tat of drums, informing all our Dales with an under-music that keeps heart alive. Uncle Robert, at seventy, rode over to Pateley Market, beyond Greenhow, and came home again through a storm that met him on the tops.

The storm is remembered to this day by those who happened to en-counter it. A gale blew bitter from nor'-east, with skelping sleet in front. Half-way between Greenhow and Hebden, Uncle Robert's horse—his hoofs balled by frozen snow—fell suddenly, rolled over, and broke his  master's leg. The victim was carried to a neighbouring farm-stead, and an hour later was in fighting trim again when they suggested he should stay there till the doctor came.

He proposed to have the leg set in his own home, or not at all, and had his way. The farm gig carried him, through bitter and increasing tempest, over and down to his Threshfield tavern. And there he lay abed for many weeks, till it chanced that Parliament dissolved and an election was sprung upon the country.

Uncle Robert was fiery in politics, as in most things. He insisted that they should take him to the polling booth; and both sides cheered him as he was driven to the door.

" How goes it with the leg, Uncle ? " asked a bystander.

" It wanted an airing—wanted it badly," said he.

He died that way, years afterwards. Knowing the end near, he got from his bed to the window overlooking Threshfield's ancient peace. The little post-office that had sent many a letter of his into the outer world—the comely houses, quick with remembrance of the folk they sheltered—the raking Greenhow slopes that strode to the further, cloud-flecked sky—these he saw, one thinks, with the clear, happy vision that death gives such stalwarts.

Threshfield rests tired men

" There'll never be another Uncle Robert in the Dale," he said. And so he died.

There will not be another. Take him for all he was—take him for all he is, a memory strong among us—that is his epitaph. There'll never be another Uncle Robert.

Threshfield rests tired men, as Burnsall does. Her many houses are in order, fragrant with rosemary for remembrance of their simple history. The rooks thrive and multiply in stately trees that guard her borders. The high, wind-clean moors look down on her sheltered hollow and save her from the worst lash of tempest.

Every unspoiled village of the Dales has its special time, when it calls to a man's heart and melts it. Threshfield's hour comes in July, as dusk settles, moist and warm, across the brooding quiet. Close at hand is the smell of hay, safely garnered into village barns. Further afield there steals the odour of wet swathes, ungathered yet, rained on and smitten by the sun alternately.

Scents have a strange power of reaching the heart, and stirring memories, but the most magical of all is waiting for one at the last homestead in the village, going Linton way—the long, quiet house with mullioned windows that have looked out on many yesterdays. There comes to you from its garden the keen, persuasive fragrance of the Yorkshire Rose—the white rose, honey-hearted, that is ours.

Threshfield's peace goes backward through the centuries to wars that built her tranquil ease. The Britons fought here. The Danes swept plundering by. The Romans brought conquest, and with it a clemency that grafted civilization on the strong northern root. Later the Scots came, rapacious as the Danes ; and later still came other Scots, who had followed Prince Charles Edward to Derby and had trudged home again with broken hearts.

One little band of these must have tramped past the Besom-Maker's house, and up the hill. On such a dusk as this, with a corncrake plaining in meadow-grass uncut as yet, you hear the limp of their bleeding feet, the cadence of their wild lament for all that might have been.

And now again the fragrance of the Yorkshire Rose brings present days to mind. Clear limned by memory of their people and their guardian hills, three villages come into mind— Threshfield here, and Linton, and Burnsall that is girdled by Wharfe River. They were ever one in sympathy, one in their comely charm. And in the midst of them is their small sister, Thorpe-in-the-Hollow, the unspoilt darling of the family.

Reek of the hay steals over Threshfield village. The corn-crake has gone to bed, but owls are busy with their hunting-cry. Quiet and fragrant, urgent with thanksgiving, the White Rose of Yorkshire speeds its message from the garden near at hand.

It is a beguiling homeland to live in, and to know by heart. That is the Rose's call to evensong.

XVI

A WAYFARING TALE

An Ancient Cave—A Rip Van Winkle of the Dale—Jammy o'
Sarah's Journey—" For Nell's Sake."

POVERTY is said to find strange bedfellows, and weather
can certainly provide one with companions odd and
unexpected. One such day returns to mind whenever I
think of pleasant Skirethorns, a hamlet neighbouring Threshfield. A sudden deluge overtook me as I came over the
Malham tops and down towards the hamlet. There was only
one real shelter from such a storm ; and, making for the cave a
field's length from the road, I found it tenanted already. A
withered, grey old man was smoking tranquilly by the light of a
farthing dip, and he greeted me with a gentle smile, as one who
had outlived doubt of strangers.

" So you know this ancient cave," he said.

" Since I was a boy."

" And that's not so long ago, measure your years by mine.
They say I'm eighty-two, but I forget all that. I'm young as
yesterday and to-morrow—especially to-morrow."

He leaned against the cave-wall, and smoked with grave content.
His face was criss-crossed everywhere with lines that life had
written on its parchment ; but his eyes glowed, even in the dim
candle-light, with a keen and happy fire.

" I used to come here often enough before your time," he
went on, " though I've wandered ever since. I was thinking,

when you stepped in, of what my father used to tell about the cave."

Oral tradition is one of my fixed and cherished hobbies, and I was alert in a moment.

" A legend ? " I prompted.

" Call it that if you like, though my father fancied it was history. He'd no book learning, you see, but just passed down,

A sheltered corner

word for word, what *his* father had told him, and so to the far-back times. What he said was that a band of Scottish men sheltered here for a night on their way back from giving more blows than they took, somewhere in the south. The Prince's men, they styled themselves, and seemed proud of a yellow-haired laddie. They wore petticoats, and talked gibberish, and were very gentle in their ways with women and children. One of them came to the inn my folk kept at Skirethorns, and frightened them nigh out of their wits with his fierce eyes and the thing he carried in his hand."

The tale absorbed me more and more, for a reason of my own.

" What did he carry in his hand ? " I asked, afraid almost to disturb his tranquil flow of memory.

" A long shaft, tall as himself, with a blade at the end of it. But, bless you, he meant no harm ! He'd had neither bite nor sup for a day, and asked only for a meal. While that was getting ready, he caught sight of a toddling bairn, and picked her up, and cried like a child himself. There was one like her, he said, waiting for him if ever he got back to a place called Skye. He didn't look like getting far. Death seemed written in his face."

There's a queer little song stirs in a man's heart at such a time. Long before rain drove me to-day into companionship with this wayfarer, a zealous opener-up of caves had found here, among the roof-droppings and litter of the years, a Scottish pike and a tinder box with a wisp of child's hair inside it. Another persistent legend of the Dale found corroboration— that a number of Prince Charles Edward's men had sheltered for the night here during the retreat from Derby.

"Let an old man talk on," said the traveller, with a smile that would have disarmed a footpad of the roads. So much went to that smile—joy in the past for its own sake, love of the present, because he was alive to share it—a wonderful, compelling charity that had seen much and forgiven much, in himself and other usual folk. " Let an old man talk. I've not been near my birthplace for a tale of years, and I'm remembering."

He asked me how Farmer So-and-So and other worthies were doing. There was an odd confusion in his mind, as if he expected everybody in the parish to remain at the same age as when he left it, awaiting his return. He had a mobile face, this Rip Van Winkle of the Dale, and it showed keen distress as little by little he understood how changed the old haunts were.

Break the news gently as I would, the death of this and that old crony touched him like a knife-thrust.

"Well," he said at last, "I reckon Greet Bank has been busy since I left. The hill of weeping—that's what my father always said it meant, because the road went down it to the burial-place." He fell to musing, but recovered by-and-by. The quaint, disarming smile returned. "I fancied I was coming *home*," he said, "and see what a fool I was for all my pains." Then, as if to go far back in time relieved him, he launched on me a surprise that took my breath away. "It's an old, ancient cave, this. They say a British Queen absconded in it once, when the world's dawn was rising."

For a moment I was tempted to smile at his turn of phrase, till some memory returned of the right good English of the Vulgate. "The prophets absconded by fifties in a cave." The stranger's speech was better than my own.

"Why did she hide?" I suggested.

"I couldn't tell you—only that the lands hereabout were thick with British camps. In my young days they were draining some boglands near the moor, and came on bones and skulls scattered all over a ten-acre field. Flint axe-heads there were, too. They were a terrible quarrelsome folk in these parts—then, as now," he added, with dry banter.

That was all; but a host of surmises sprang suddenly to view. These uplands above Skirethorns—gaunt, rock-strewn wilds— had their counterpart right up the Dale. All are natural fortresses for hard-pressed men. Over above Kettlewell, undying rumour says that the British fought a harsh battle, and were scattered. And the British Queen who hid in Skire-thorns cave—was she some northern Boadicea, rallying broken fighters? And was the last, forlorn stand of all made on the edge of the moor above, where bones and skulls were scattered all over a ten-acre field? In a moment this dreamer of old dreams had set one's vagabond fancy roaming along royal highways. Not many miles over the tops that hide us from Yoredale, a Scottish Queen tasted liberty for two hours of a captivity that was to end at Fotheringay. Through that mad, headlong gallop she shared with Kit Norton, she, too, must have been planning a last stand of her leal warriors against an overpowering foe. And here in the cave some of the Prince's men had halted on their bleak journey north from Derby—

Wayside Peace

defeated, not in battle, but in the council-chamber of their own Highland chieftains. Yet they, too, were thinking of the battle promised them in Scotland. Hope stayed with them. And the end of that was Culloden. How fared it with the British Queen whose feet had rested where ours stood to-day? Perhaps fate was kinder to her than to the Stuart race. She died, maybe, leading her folk and not knowing that they and she were doomed.

"Thinking backward, too, are you?" said the little, old man with a face like criss-cross parchment. He had taken another farthing dip from his pocket and lit it. "It brings a look there's no mistaking—but you're young for that sort of pastime."

The rain ended as suddenly as it had come, and we stepped out presently into hot sunlight and a reek of steaming mist.

" This is the homeland back again at last," laughed my wayfarer. " Dale's weather never did anything by halves."

Yet the man was shaken. By what he said and left unsaid on our way down the track, more like a bouldered stream-bed than a road, I knew that he, too, was following a royal highway—of sick defeat borne with rugged, quiet distinction. And presently the question I feared was asked me—asked piteously, as a lost child might crave protection from its loneliness. We had come to the croft, full of grazing sheep, where the Skirethorns inn stood once. He looked for wood-smoke curling up from grey chimney-stacks—for horses tethered to the rings on either side of the door, while their masters drank ripe ale inside and stable-boys were whistling in the yard. He stood for awhile stock-still, like one in nightmare, and passed a hand across tired eyes. And then the question came.

" Where's the old, ramshackle homestead gone ? "

" Into neighbouring barns. There was no need of an inn this side of Malham, so they said. So it died, and fell to bits."

That roused him from his grief.

" ' They say ' was always a town-bred fool. What do they know of Malham weather and drovers coming to my father's door—men and sheep foredone and sweating after a trudge through drifts of swirling snow ? And there's no welcome now for such as they."

Memory had him in thrall again. Though we stood in the hot sun-glow, and the breeze was soft, I shivered as he painted winter on the Malham Fells. Drovers on foot with their ewes, mounted yeomen, had come half-dead, at one time and another, to his father's inn—sometimes by day, when a blizzard leaped from the north-east at them and hid sky and pastures before they reached Malham gate and the road that led them between guardian walls to Skirethorns—sometimes by night. They had left Malham with their flocks in clouded moonlight, enough to show them the remembered track. On the tops they came into windless snow, heavy, wet, and clinging; and in a moment they were lost. When their own instinct failed, they trusted for direction to their dogs, and muddled down, somehow, to Skirethorns and its friendly tavern.

"Not needed, the old inn?" he said, at the end of one of these heroic tales, fast following each other. "Not needed, because there's another at Threshfield, barely a half-mile off? Aye, but wiseacres should remember that a road has two ends to it—and I'll tell you what happened to Jammy o' Sarah's, as we always called him."

The road that led between guardian walls to Skirethorns

This native, come back to the old that was desolately new, was lifted out of himself. The cold negation of the present urged him to kindle ancient fires afresh and warm both hands at them. He told his tale better than he knew, and for his moment was kin to the world's great artists.

"Jammy o' Sarah's was a drover bred and born. He never bothered with marriage and ties o' that sort. You might say he doted on the sheep and cattle he drove to market for other men to sell and buy—but specially on sheep. It was his boast that he'd never lost one to his tally in all his years of droving. But he came near it on a night gone by."

Into the croft where once the inn had been, a farm-lad

slouched, driving a flock of sheep with their half-grown lambs, bleating together in a wild confusion.

"Their din's naught," said the wayfarer—"naught at all, compared with the uproar I heard once in this same place. Jammy the drover had set out from Malham in a scud of hail, and they warned him not to go with his ewes. Worse would be waiting for him on the heights, they said. But Jammy only answered that he'd given his word to get his flock over hill by a certain time, and go he would. Obstinate, some named him. Others called him faithful. But by-names are of lile account. It was what Jammy o' Sarah's did one night that has settled into my mind." A light was in his eyes—a light that crosses a boy's face when he reads a book by fire-glow and its hero slays his dragons. "It was not very out of the usual, so Jammy seemed to think afterwards. But for me—Lord only knows how often I think of him. When weather snarls at me, Jammy o' Sarah's came through worse than this, say I to myself, and just trudge forward."

His tale was crisp and vivid. It told how Jammy started from Malham with his dog Tinker and fifty sheep that he'd promised to bring into fold at Skirethorns before nightfall. The wind had been nagging for three days from the north-east, and the scuds of hail increased. He was told he was mad to take the journey. This dry, wandering sort of snow would "do its damnedest to him" before he got over-fell. To all persuasion Jammy answered that he'd promised to get the ewes over, and a bargain was a bargain. So then, knowing him, they let him go. The King himself could not have kept him from the journey—supposing His Majesty had happened to be in Malham at the moment, which was not very likely.

Jammy took the road with his flock; and as they came to Gordale Brigg, the worst thing that can happen to a man in the way of storm drove full at them. The wind yelped out of the

frozen wastes above and brought a snow-scud—little, sharp
arrows that hid sky and land, and broke the skin on a man's face,
or seemed to do. As he got further up, with eyelids half drawn
down to resist the snow-knives—blundering his way forward
and touching the wall on either hand at times for guidance—the
sky grew clear again. He came to Mastiles Lane, and the wind
shifted suddenly to south-west, with a smell of violets in it, as of
spring to come. So then Jammy took great heart. He told
himself that thaw was coming fast, and that he would have the
laugh, after all, of the wiseacres at Malham.

Thaw did come, with driving sheets of rain, and it lasted
half an hour, or less—just long enough to let him get into the
middle of the trackless pastures that lay between Mastiles Lane
and the road down to Skirethorns. Then it blew north-east
again, and snow came in earnest. Thick, close-packed flakes
were harried by a gale that bit to the bone's marrow. He groped
his way to a wall and followed it by touch, thinking it was the
fence that ran this side of the Druid's Altar Stones and on to the
gate he sought. When the wind backed to south for another
spell and the sun got through, he found the wall had led him to
the top of the high fells away towards Kilnsey. So they took
their bearings afresh, he and his shivering dog, and saw the
fence they needed, and made for it. Before they reached its
solid guidance, the sunlight was tattered to bits and the snow hid
all but the ground close under their feet.

And so the whole journey went. If it had been one ceaseless
blizzard, Tinker and he between them would have puzzled a
way through by instinct. What hindered them to the verge of
panic was the ceaseless chop-and-change from snow to rain and
back to needle-sleet. The sheep sent up a never-ending, wild
lament, hard to bear. And small wonder, for alternate rain and
snow, frozen by the wind, had burdened their fleeces till they
could scarcely trudge through the gathering drifts. There had

been little snow in sheltered Skirethorns; and folk looking from the inn-parlour marvelled to see a whitened drover and a ghostly dog shepherding a flock of icicles.

" My father came out," the wayfarer goes on, " and Jammy o' Sarah's was thawing a bit by then, so he could know who he was. ' You've brought the ewes, as you promised,' said my father. ' Ay,' said Jammy. ' But it's been what you might call a comfortless journey.' And with that he dropped where he stood, like a plummet. And it would have been Kingdom-Come for Jammy if they hadn't dolloped him with enough rum to kill a weaker man."

Towards the high fells

My Rip Van Winkle takes a last glance at the croft that once had known his homestead, and we jog together down the lane. Wild-rose and honeysuckle are rife with fragrance, the hot sun drinking the rain from their blossoms. It is hard to believe it is summer, for one has been spirited away to many a winter's storm and mixed weather on the Malham tops. The wayfarer halts suddenly as we turn the bend where a great clump of bushes stands between the highway and the wall, and glances at the road.

" Did you ever come here on the second day of January ? " he asks abruptly. " But I've been away a long while—longer than I thought—it's all forgotten, doubtless."

Not quite forgotten. Memory returns of a tale told long ago ;

and with that phantom story comes recollection, too, of the
nursery at home, of flame and shadows chasing each other across
the pictured walls, of an old nurse lulling me to sleep with every
fearsome story of the countryside she could draw upon.
Memory of her is poignant, somehow—friendly and deep-seated,
heralding the advent of my mother, who came with a sharp,
"Nurse, do you want to nightmare the child?" And I can hear
again the nurse's quick rejoinder, " I was telling him a bonnie
tale, ma'am, of the maid murdered by a man in Skirethorns Lane.
He hid her body in the thicket, he did, and they found her when
the leaves were shed. And ever since, on the second day o' the
New Year, there's a running pool o' crimson starts up across the
road." "Oh, hush, Tabitha!" comes the protest. And nurse
answers, " Hush for why? Lads thrive on such old bed-
time tales."

She was right. Here on the haunted spot itself I recall the
shiver of delight and fear that sent me into sound and dreamless
sleep. For the boy is made as he's made, and nothing alters
that. The wayfarer's voice rouses me from memories, as he
traces a pattern in the roadway with his stick. If his account of
the haunting is less vivid than the nurse's " running pool of crimson," it carries with it a strange sense of conviction.

" You hear naught. And you see naught, except a blood-
stain that comes out on the road—shape of a heart, as I'm drawing it here in the dust. I've not seen it myself, having no gift
that way ; but I've talked with a few that have. Every second of
January it's there, just before dusk comes on."

" What was the story? " I ask, recalling only vague, con-
tradictory legends.

" Simple enough, and full enough o' grief. Poor Nell !
She'd good looks enough to have shared with two or three other
maids, and never missed 'em. And of course the men were wild
for her ; and of course she knew it. There was no harm in her,

you understand ; but she made a frolic of her lovers, putting one against another. Then the right lad came. She couldn't stop her teasing ways, even then—maddened him with jealousy, here where I'm talking. And before he knew, his hands were at her throat. and afterwards he hid her in the bushes. Poor Nell ! She'd never learned that men are kittle folk to play with when they're in love."

The man falls into moody silence as we journey forward, and at the Threshfield corner, where the four grey roads stride out into lands of old romance, memories tug at his heart. He is shaken by a storm of retrospect. Tears I'm ashamed to catch a glimpse of are held back.

"How's Mary, who keeps the Fountaine Inn at Linton ? I'm jogging over for a crack about the bygone times."

When the news was broken that she, like many another, had crossed the Border, his heart died in him for a moment. Then he recovered, with a game hardihood that was instinct in the man.

"To be sure, I'm getting old, though I fancy myself young at times. But I'd like to have had a gossip with Mary. She knew poor Nell."

So then it grew clear, somehow, that his long years of exile had been for Nell's sake. His return was for her sake. This way-worn traveller, without any trappings of the picturesque, was, after all, the rarest of all beings—a poet whose love had not faltered or grown weary. The only price he asked for his caring was to remember Nell—to picture Heaven knew what of all he could have given her, if she had known.

When we reach the gate that opens on a wide, green lane, pointing straight to the summer-haze above old Simon's Seat, he says good-bye, with a smile dragged up from the depths of tragedy.

"It doesn't do to come back—not to come back to the living. So I'll just step down to Linton kirkyard, where my dead lie."

I watched him go, till the last of his frail body winked out, as it were, against the bluff, far-away bulk of the up-striding fells. And, somehow, drive out fancy as I may, the thought recurs that he found Nell in the churchyard—as he had seen her through his long, faithful pilgrimage.

XVII

GIRSTON

The Mystery of the Musk—Doctor Petty and Tom Lee—Tom Airey—
A Village Theatre—Harriet Mellon.

GRASSINGTON is its modern title, but to hear a native speak of it as Girston is to be sure at once of its true name. And Garr's End, in the village itself, gives confirmation. Garr was its overlord once on a day, and Garr's Town has become, by a natural turn of folk-speech, just Girston. No name could fit the village half as well. Crisp and strong, it is the place itself, somehow. Its street, narrow and steep, goes up to the cobbled market-square, and narrows again between the house-fronts till it strides into the free winds of the pasture lands above. Wrinkled, winding alleys branch everywhere, as the whim takes them. Pursuing these, you happen, when least expecting it, on a farmstead and the sweet breath of cattle. The farm was there before the village, and does not mean to budge.

You will happen, too, on garden-strips in front of cottage windows. There seems no room for them in this village of the cobbled streets; but they abide and flourish, and have done since the oldest man in Girston remembers gillifers and rock-roses springing year by year from these well-tended gardens. The elders wag their heads, however, about the friendly little musk that still ramps everywhere among the stones, with its flowers of golden-yellow. The musk has no fragrance nowadays, they say. And that is not a fable of disgruntled ancients, finding all wrong with younger times. Through the whole length of England gardeners have the same plaint ; and none can explain the mystery. Only the little lady encountered in an earlier chapter—she who has the gift of " sensing " vanished gardens—seems left to enjoy the bygone fragrance. These gardens, tiny as they are, temper Girston's ruggedness, and explain much of it. Under its people's quiet and unresponsive front, there is friend-

Grassington is its modern title

ship waiting, and heart-whole welcome. But you have to win it, as they and their sires have won foothold on a hillside bleak to every wind that blows.

Girston, of all the Wharfedale villages, speaks most plainly of the past fights the British made among these northern hills. It takes no shelter from the hollows, but looks from its gnarled old streets for foemen to be met. The lands above are thick with bones of warriors fallen in defence of the last fortresses. That was before ever a stone of the present village was reared in place ; but its builders heard, one fancies, the voices of fighting men whose feet had passed that way lang-syne. A village of strong personality, that grips one with wayward, subtle power—a village whose later story is full of odd happenings and of sharp changes that leave it, somehow, still unchanged—that is Girston.

There's the tale of Doctor Petty and Tom Lee, the village blacksmith. No drama invented by man's fancy could have a more downright, savage cogency than this thing that happened. The doctor was a bluff, cheery practitioner who healed more ailments by a laugh and a slap on the back than ever his physic did. Tom Lee, the brawniest man in the parish and feared by all, found smithy-work too slow a means of livelihood. Robberies began to be noised abroad, but none dared name the culprit, though they knew him. Lee went too far at last. There was a "running postman" then between Greenhow's mines and Girston, carrying money, and Lee lay in wait for him at the top of the last hill down to Hebden. The postman smashed Lee to a jelly, and went free with what he carried.

Lee had bullied the countryside with entire immunity till now. Sorry for himself, as only bullies can be, he took his wounds to Doctor Petty, who patched him up and sent him about his business with a sharp warning that he had better mend his evil ways. The whole succeeding tragedy took its first, dim shape in Lee's brain when Doctor Petty sounded that warning note. Bruised and battered, thwarted in his robbery, the wastrel was in evil mood. Suspicion stirred in him. He had been compelled to share his secret, and the doctor might bring him to the gibbet that was then the penalty for highwaying. The doctor himself gave no thought to this side of the matter. Much as he longed to see the countryside freed of its worst reprobate, it did not occur to him as possible to betray a confidence shared by patient and physician. But Tom Lee nursed suspicion till it became a mania. The wilder his drinking bouts, the more surely his grievance " settled in." The black dog was on his shoulders, as his neighbours had it, and he was ripe for any mischief.

Inevitably the story finds Lee drinking in the Kilnsey tavern, a few miles away from Girston, just when Doctor Petty drew rein there on his way home from a long round up-Dale. Lee snarled at the doctor, who was tired and in no mood for this sort of welcome; and when the other let his foul tongue loose in earnest, Petty nodded briskly at him.

"Tom Lee," he said, "d'ye never glimpse the halter that's itching for your neck?"

With that he went out to his horse, tethered to the ring at the inn-door, and the landlady followed him.

"I'm glad you gave him tit for tat, doctor," she said. "Lord knows it's time somebody stood up to that outrageous vagabones. He's putting the whole Dale in a fright."

"He'll stumble over himself going home, one of these dark nights," laughed the doctor, his good-humour to the fore again—"stumble over himself—break his neck that way, and rob the halter. He'll rob to the end, you understand."

She laughed with him, and went in for the stirrup-cup, and put the glass into his hands as he stood on the threshold. Perhaps her hand trembled, for she had long been in fear of Tom Lee, and he was still inside her inn. At any rate, the glass fell to the stone floor, and lay there—unbroken. Even the doctor blanched a little. He had known the Dale too long not to have gathered its superstitions close into his fibres. For a glass to fall and be broken—that mattered little—but all men knew what this other happening meant.

"Ride home with care," pleaded the landlady.

Petty shook himself free of the omen, nodded cheerily, and swung his big weight into the saddle. Crossing Wharfe into Coniston village, he stayed there some while with a patient; and Tom Lee, who came that way on foot soon after, saw the doctor's horse standing outside the sick man's door. The black dog was on his shoulders again, and the resolve long-forming took sudden shape as he hurried forward on the Girston road.

Dusk was falling when Doctor Petty rode slowly home. The horse and rider were always weary at the end of their up-Dale journeys, and Petty—thinking doubtless of the warm hearth and cosy meal awaiting him—rode into the shadows of Grass Wood. Lee, crouching at the wall-side, with a cudgel ready to hand, leapt out and struck him down. The horse galloped in mad panic for its stable. Lee was sobered now. The doctor was the best-loved man in Wharfedale, proved long ago by many roads of kindliness and skill. Lee knew that half Girston would be out in search as soon as news spread of the riderless horse. He stooped to drag the body into hiding; but the doctor was not done with yet. Great strength, tenacity to live, asserted themselves, as of old. He was able, in the last spurt before death, to clutch Lee by the throat and force him down. And that was the end of Doctor Petty—a fighting end, as he would have wished.

A little lad, belated on the road, watched it all; and when the boy grew out of the horror of it all, years afterwards, he told what he had seen; and that is how we know one part of the story. Lee dragged his victim far into the wood, where the brackens grew tall beneath the trees, and got home to find the hue-and-cry sounding everywhere through Girston's streets. His wife had to be told, and his apprentice; for both were there when he came to the smithy house in bloodstained clothes. He bound them to secrecy by appalling oaths. Then his long penance-time—and theirs—began.

They helped him, at stark midnight of the next day, to drag the body through the wood, and up on to the open moor. They worked with pick and shovel, till the dead man lay deep under peat. And that gave Tom Lee a week's ease of mind. Then he heard a man talking in the village inn of the strange power that moorland peat-soil had to embalm a body given to its care. Again Lee fell into heedless panic; and a few nights later two lovers, lingering in the moonlight under Loup Scar, hard by Burnsall village, heard a splash and saw a man's figure on the cliff above.

That was the beginning of the end for Tom Lee. The lovers summoned help. What they found in Wharfe River, and tracing of the way its bearer came to Loup Scar, hanged Lee at the finish. They say his gibbet-irons are buried on the little hill that looks over Girston Brigg— the beautiful, grey bridge that had carried Doctor Petty on many an errand of mercy.

A grim tale enough. Yet there are men who deride the superstition that makes folk afraid to go through

Loup Scar

Grass Wood near dusk at the place where the doctor made his end, fighting to the last. Let them go alone and take their chance of hearing frenzied hoof-beats tear up and down the Girston Road, as his horse goes riderless again. Let them stand rooted to the spot, as the belated lad stood long ago, and watch and hear it all—if it happens that they care to stay.

This far-off story of Tom Lee has gripped the imagination of succeeding generations. Lee, in his own way, has captured something of the dour romance attaching to Eugene Aram, a murderer more notable. But Girston's memories are threaded by many a happier tale. To think of Tom Airey, for instance, is to conjure up a vision of the times when men had heart to jest and be merry, had leisure for the day's work and for much beside.

Airey, the village postmaster, had known what it meant to carry the mail on foot to Skipton, nine miles away, in any sort of weather, and to walk the nine miles back. Later, he went on horseback, and afterwards drove a gig that developed by-and-by into a roomy trap. That conveyance was the beginning of a tradition strong amongst us still. Soon it grew to be known as " The Mail," and old affection has gathered round its name. It carried what Tom Airey named " Royalty's goods," but letters were not its only passengers. Folk learned soon what it meant to travel the Skipton Road that winds between the high fells and the moors—to travel it behind a pair of horses, Tom Airey handling the reins and turning often to explain how good it was to be alive. The Mail grew to be the daily link between up-Dale villages and their market town. It carried gossip south and brought it north again—served indeed as the news-sheet of the countryside. The driver sped greetings by word of mouth from friend to friend. Often he picked up a foot-sore traveller who obviously had no money for his fare—silenced his question with a bluff, " That's all right. The Mail's half empty, and you'll help to balance her." His memory was a thing to marvel at, and a mail-driver of later days explained it with cheery clearness as we drove together up the road.

" There's no use in trusting by halves. If I'd a notebook, and scribbled down all they told me—John Metcalfe needing a pair o' boots, and Wiseman's lass wanting a ribbon matched, and what all—the Mail would never get into Skipton till the next day. So I says to memory, ' Stick to 'un like a bull-dog, lad.' And memory sticks."

Tom Airey fathered them all—these drivers of the Mail that

brought ripe fellowship from Skipton Town to Buckden in the hills. His epitaph is instinct in the winds that blow about the Road, in the fells that break into foam of hawthorn bloom when June arrives, a maiden in her bridal-gear. Even yet you find his name remembered on the lusty road that branches, left and right, to Langstrothdale and Hubberholme.

Tom Airey has another claim on our remembrance. He had a passion for the stage, and was a sound actor himself, with the

A Coniston sheep-washing

gift of inspiring others to enthusiasm. Their theatre was a roomy barn, and they were healthily ambitious, as is proved by Airey's own log-book of the plays they tackled without thought of failure. To handle that book, to turn its pages, is to be transported into a world of high adventure; for Airey would have nothing of clumsy farces and the reward of loud guffaws. Into this village life of the drama two strolling players came. They were " barn-stormers "—professionals who played for hire in just such theatres as Airey had for his only stage. Skipton had then a tiny theatre known as the Hole in the Wall, and it was after a " season " there that these two players drifted up to Girston and joined Airey's company. One of the' two was

Edmund Kean, the other Harriet Mellon, and both were destined for high places, as the world knows by this time. Miss Mellon, apart altogether from her power as an actress, was possessed of most singular charm and kindliness. Her personality was compelling enough to capture the heart of Coutts, the banker, and after his death the Duke of St. Albans claimed her hand in marriage.

Tom Airey was proud of these two. He had shared the same rustic boards with them, had known they would go far; and his tales of old theatre days in Girston were haloed by eager hero-worship. The Duke of Devonshire, who had landed interest in the mines and woods, was an occasional visitor to the village, and word would be brought to Airey that the Duke meant to see his play that night. A semi-royal box was forthwith erected, of boards covered with brown paper, and the Duke ushered into it with becoming ceremony.

" The Girston folk thought it a great condescension for His Grace to look in," Airey would say in after years, " but I told 'em to bide till two of ours came to their own. There were a good few dukes about, but only one Edmund Kean, and never another Harriet Mellon."

It tickled Airey's humour when he heard that his fellow-player of old times was a duchess, as well as the first actress of the day.

" She can hob-nob with our Duke at his own game now," he would say; "but what sort of show would *he* make if he had to take the boards ? "

Airey had a curious story of Harriet Mellon. The child of strolling players, she was left in the bedroom of a tavern by her mother, who was acting in the country town. The landlady, left in charge, had found the bairn asleep and had tip-toed out for fear of waking her. The room was on the ground-floor. Above it was the graveyard of an ancient church, and the wet mould of centuries, breaking through the inn-wall at last, roused the sleeping child. The lamp at the far end of the chamber showed her a pile of earth and bones and skulls ; and she shrieked aloud for help.

Sometimes, after playing in the Girston Theatre, Harriet Mellon " would lose herself," as Airey put it, and sob and cry beside his hearth in utter panic. Then she would laugh through the tears, and explain how the disastrous happening of her childhood returned to her when she was overwrought. And he told her— he, who knew more of acting than he could follow through himself—to be content. In childhood, when the mould and the dead bones broke across her sleep, she had learned from anguish how to hold folk's hearts in later years.

" You'll go far, little Harriet," this sagacious counsellor would say.

" I feel weak and small to-night," she would answer, with a wistful smile.

" Ay, but I'm thinking of to-morrow, lass."

Her to-morrow came at flood, and Airey delighted in one story of her later years. She returned in prosperity and state to Skipton, glanced in to see if the Hole in the Wall theatre was still there, and went to other shrines of memory. Especially she tried to find Miss Rodwell, who had played with her in the Girston days of barn-storming—little Rodwell, settled sedately long ago as a dressmaker in the town. She did not find her until her return to the Devonshire Hotel, where her old friend was waiting.

" I ventured to call, Your Grace," said Harriet, all in a twitter.

The Duchess broke into the other's protestations by embracing her with fervour. Then she held her at arm's length, to see how the years had used her.

" *Ventured* to call ? And I'm ' My Grace,' am I ? Little Rodwell, how good those old days were."

No more than that you got from Airey—just the tale, without a weak line anywhere in the picture it conjures to one's mind.

Bleak as the village stands to weather that can bite deep, it has learned how to make music out of hardship; and its life has been full of odd colour and romance. Once it was known as Silver Town, because they found lead on the moors, and miners reaped a bigger wage from under soil than ever the farmers did from surface crops. It was then the Cornish men settled in—born miners, of the Celtic breed, and far-off cousins to the early Britons who made their last stand in the Dale. Their broken cottages still hug the ruined mine-shafts on the moor, and there are times when the sun sinks red in thunder, and elfin lights play up and down this dead land that remembers old prosperity. Silver Town below jogs on; but at this hour the ghosts of old miners fret, because for them there is no more going down to peril of the labour that called them with a piping, eager song.

Not long ago, as the Dale counts age, a stream flowed across Girston's street, and it was an honoured custom that there should be dancing on its bridge whenever a wedding happened. Tom Airey's grand-daughter, happily, is with us still, and has a power all her own of breaking through the mists of yesterday. She loves specially the picture of her mother's wedding, as the dame described it in her later years. A simple picture, arresting in its gaiety. There is the journey to Linton church of groom and bride, the gathering of villagers from every corner of a wide-flung parish, the journey back to Girston, preceded by a fiddler who knew how to coax laughter from the strings. Then came the bridal-feast, and after that the dancing at the bridge. Fourteen couples shared the dance. Gradely men, and maidens limber as the Dale could make them, trod to and fro in their silver-buckled shoes. The bridge had room only for one couple at a time, and over the stream they footed it, in a faster and a faster whirl. The chattering stream and the twinkling feet—you see and hear them when Tom Airey's grand-daughter lives back into the olden days.

Like all the clustered villages of Wharfe, at this stage of the
river's journey, Girston has its foundations deep in lore of
Fountains Abbey. So has the Hall—the oldest house, unless it
is my own at Linton, in the long Dale. If you go by the field-
way down to Girston Brigg—grey as the hills themselves—you
can look down Dale, and see only houses that link the elder
days to ours. There's the house by the bridge, with its high-
pitched roof. It was a pilgrims' rest-house once, where wayfarers halted for the night on their long journey out to Fountains.

Houses that link the elder days to ours

At the garden-foot is the Lady Well, its waters blessed since
mediæval days. Beyond the house of the steep-pitched gable
is another, old in every line. And nobody knows its story. A
beguiling house, that seems to have tales to tell, if one could only
get at them. Beyond again is the Elizabethan school and the
quiet hollow where the corn-mill stands that gave shelter once to
Emily Norton. Beyond once again—raking up and down, a
twisted ribbon between the pastures and the wooded knolls—the
grey track winds to Thorpe-in-the-Hollow. On the far moor-crest
old Simon's Seat stands swart against a dove-grey sky and looks
down upon this vale of sheer enchantment. Wharfe, in all her
wanderings, has no happier sweep of landscape than Girston's
field-path gives you. It stirs the heart, and kindles fancy ; and
the heron, drifting overhead on wide, majestic pinions, is its
true interpreter.

XVIII

A CHAPTER ON WEATHER

" Lile Scant-Wit "—Dalesmen Bred out of Weather—A Challenge—The Secret Sign—The Shepherd.

WEATHER is the high priest of fellowship among Dalesfolk. Men with a long quarrel unhealed have been driven to speech with one another because they met on some lonely road and the day called for comment. It may be a June morning of glamour almost unbelievable, or a winter's dusk when sleet comes nipping down the north-east gale. They exchange a greeting for the first time in many years ; and thereafter it is absurd not to continue the good habit. Mere personal gossip is dwarfed always on the highlands 'by weather, and the backslidings of neighbour-folk are forgotten when work is up about the lands. If ploughing is to be done, the skies are sought with anxious glance in hope of sun and a drying wind. When winter rages out of the north-east, and snows pack up in big, green-grey clouds before they shroud the pastures, farmers think of the coming journeys through stress and storm in search of foundered sheep. The lasses, on their wedding morns, peep out from shy, maiden casements to ask if the sun will shine on them. The rooks come after storm, swinging on the tree-tops to learn what damage it has done to the nests where they hope to rear other families next spring.

Weather is the prime personality of the Dale. It can sour the spirit in a man, or lift his soul to melody. Is it any wonder that the prophets accounted of most honour among us are those wise in weather-lore ? There is a constantly recurring belief among our people that "scant-wit laddies"—those, in gentler phrase, " not just like other folk "—have a supreme instinct for weather prophecy. So strong was this faith, indeed, almost in one's own time here, that the advice of such was sought eagerly whenever a farmer had to make serious and deliberate choice. If a spell of fair weather came after long rains in June, and it was doubtful if it would last until the hay was won, they consulted " lile scant-wit." If a scud of snow whitened the pastures in mid-winter, and they wondered if there was need to bring the sheep down from the fells, they ran for guidance to the same source of inspiration.

For my own part, I have always sought guidance from the older race of farmers, and have profited amazingly ; but the most skilled in the craft, to my mind, was Jonathan Sturt, as we will name him. He drove the horse mail for half his life-time—the good ramshackle 'bus that took letters from Skipton to outlying villages on the route to Buckden. Day in, day out, he followed the road, and missed it only twice—once when he married, and once when the first of his many children " had to be christened proper like, though he squealed to a right good tune when parson took him in hand."

Jonathan, of the men I've known in the Dale, was nearest to its true, inmost heart. Dawn and dusk, for many of the year's months, were known to him, as he took his team of two to Skipton in the morning and returned at night. Then the long days of March strode out, silvering the fells with a keen and eager radiance. He needed headlights no longer for his 'bus, with their troublesome oil-wicks that yielded every mile or so to a gust of sudden wind. His soul grew blithe as the days lengthened. He would talk as one sat beside him—talk of the wonderful things he saw when spring strode into summer down and up the Dale. That was the secret of his undying youth, I fancy. Nothing that happened along the Road staled. The rising of a heron, the first break of blossom-foam on wayside hawthorns, or greening of the brackens on the moors far up above—all were new to him, full of surprise and wonder as if he saw them for the first time. It was he who pulled up one spring morning to show me a clump of white violets growing in the hedge-bottom.

" Nobody knows how they came there, or who planted them," said he, with a cheery flourish of his whip. " There's not another clump from this to Langstrothdale."

The next moment, as we jogged forward, he was deep in talk of men and women of the Dale. Slander, or gossip of the baser sort, had no interest for him. Reared among lonely hill-spaces, he knew the strength and foibles of a people, individual, strong, obstinate in love or hate. It never occurred to him to judge them. He left that sort of folly to weaker minds. And in the result—looking back on all the journeys I shared with Jonathan—there comes to me so complete a picture of the Dale that I can only marvel and be glad. Folk I have known in the scattered farmsteads are interpreted the clearer by what he told of them and of their ancestors, till one cannot distinguish between the limestone fells and those who were reared among their slopes and stony corries. All are one with the roving breeze and the over-watching sky.

" Dalesmen are bred out o' weather," said Jonathan once, as we went with His Majesty's mails up the dappled April road. " It stands to sense, doesn't it, that a man has to be up and doing when one minute nor'-east snow clouts at his lugs, and the next he's sweating in the sun ? The weak die off ; and the lusty sort live to a kittlesome, green old age."

So it all comes back to weather, and none but the Dalesman understands the wonderful zest and subtlety of such a hobby truly pursued. The Dale varies so constantly—here a broad valley, narrowing suddenly between close, overhanging hills, and widening to broad straths again—that its storms gather sharply to a head and go as swiftly. Between Burnsall and Arncliffe, little more than ten miles apart, the year's rainfall half doubles itself because of the great, rough-shouldered bulk of Arncliffe Clouder that splits the valley and " draws the skies down," as the saying is. A deluge may be in process on each side of the Clouder when lower down the sun is hot on tired pastures. In June one may waken to a land white with snow, and before noon see trees winking the last of their burden away in shimmering, gently-falling rain. There's beguilement in this infinite variety, and those who survive find a lusty pride in the best and the worst the Dale can do to them. They find, too, a curious and growing passion for weather-prophecy, till they learn to add up the hosts of little signs that, in the bulk, mean much.

Jonathan Sturt, as I have said, was a man skilled beyond belief in this pastime. If you asked him what was to be doing soon—rain or shine—he took a leisurely glance at the hills and the sky. Then he told you what would happen. Jonathan had no cold, immortal light of infallibility about him, and erred at times; but that only served as background to his amazing accuracies. From him I learned so much that presently I began to flutter my own untried pinions, and made great prophecies; and the wind raved out of Amerdale and over Arncliffe Clouder, packed with snow and hail, when I had foretold sunshine and moist airs. From such falls I got up with chastened spirit, and went to work in earnest about this business of the weather. All that Jonathan could teach me I gathered up, and wise old farmers smiled indulgently when I sought for their own readings of the sky.

" You'll never learn to put all the two-and-twos together and make 'em four," they would say. " We can scarce do it ourselves."

It was a challenge. The daft, contrary weather was a challenge. I took it up. Shooting over rough pastures, riding up the Dale, walking the high moorlands, I grew constantly more intimate with weather, and found her like a maid who baffles a wooer, yet lures him on. The first callow faith I had to shed was the belief that rain is foretold always when the hills draw near and one can see every wall and furrow of the distant slopes. It foretells broken skies, if the wind is on the west side of north ; but otherwise it spells continuity of dry weather that may soon bring drought to lean, scant-soiled acres. Yet neither of these prophecies is to be depended on, unless one knows how long the wind has been in its present quarter and how often it has boxed the compass between this and yesterday. The whole affair grows more difficult as one moves into the higher regions of prophecy ; and Jonathan Sturt was easily first among us. He would play on weather-tokens as on an instrument of many strings, with a master's sure and radiant touch.

But his disciple—a novice once—discovered something unknown to Jonathan. How or when the secret first disclosed itself, I cannot remember ; but afterwards I held it safe. It was a portent that foretold always the break-up of frost. Year by year I tested it, and found it so trusty that at last I put it to the extreme test. Liberty may be taken to dwell on that bygone episode, as if one told the tale of a six-pounder lured from some ancient trout pool, or of a long, happy shot at flighting geese. To this day I take a childish pride in the adventure.

Snow fell in October that year, and kept going and coming, never away for long, till near Christmas it fell in bitter earnest, driven by crying wolf-packs of the wind. As fast as it was piled into drifts, it froze, until the whole land was one sea of crusted billows ; and for a week the tempest yelped and whined. The snows ceased then, and the wind was tired for awhile. Near sunset—by the clock, though no sun had been seen all day—I went crunching up the lane to Thorpe-in-the-Hollow, dragging a country-made sleigh in search of the one diversion left in a shrouded countryside. Southward, east and north, there was truce, but never a hint of real peace to come. The clouds gathered, rank after sullen rank, shot through and through by the grey-green light that chills the heart in a man. What breeze there was bit at one with shrewish spite. But in the west my token showed—showed so plainly that it startled me. It seemed not possible, somehow ; but it was there, and it persisted.

" Taking in signs of the weather ? " growled a voice behind me. " Well, there's a plenty to go by."

Old Anthony Helm had come up behind me. His fine, clean-shaven face was reddened to a beetroot hue, but the cold had not killed the cheery twinkle in his eyes.

" Plenty," I agreed.

" And what d'ye make of it ? "

Faith was asked of me—unswerving faith—and his challenge brought it out.

" There'll be rain between this and dawn, Anthony—heavy rain."

He regarded me for a moment with genial pity, hard to bear.

" To be sure, you're young to weather. You haven't taken a glance about you, maybe ? "

" Yes—just a glance or two."

" Well, all I know is that the last time this sort o' blight came near Christmas, it went on till March, till no walls were left. The drifts were piled that high you could walk from Thorpe to Burnsall without ever breaking step on frozen snow."

" This time there'll be rain," I said, with happy obstinacy.

Anthony Helm nodded a grave farewell, doubting my sanity, and whistled to the dog that was nosing out friendly odours from my clothes. And I went home a little afraid of the adventure now. In the middle of that night I woke to hear the drip and gurgle of soft rain, and turned with a sigh of sheer content. Vanity lingers close to all prophets, as to other men. I had pitted my faith in one weather token against the tried wisdom of the Dale. And it was raining.

When the next day I went about the parish, with exultant modesty, the farmers were grave as they saluted me. Snow-broth was cold under our feet, and from the hills came the roar of many waters, loosened by sudden and persistent thaw.

Storm paints the wild lands with a wizard's brush

" Anthony Helm said you foretold it," was the burden of their greeting. " How did you know ? "

I kept that secret from them, like a cherished thing, not to be shared with others ; and afterwards they began to worry me whenever weather-lore was needed. I had become, it seemed, the "lile scant-wit" of the parish, needed at every turn. It is so simple a secret, after all. There's nothing spectacular about it, and my only wonder is that the token has escaped so many wiser folk. The wind may be where you like, and packed with what Jonathan Sturt was wont to name " any sort o' devilment." Everything may point to blizzards and snow that freezes as it falls. It does not matter, if at sunset a little patch of warmth

steals through the western snow-clouds. It is not easy to tell
its colour—a rosy salmon-pink describes it best, perhaps—but it
is unmistakable. The harsher the sky about this island of good
hope, the sooner thaw and rain will come. I cannot explain the
portent. I only know that, out of the welter of many weather
prophecies, this one emerges always triumphant and secure.

Apart from this pastime of foretelling its vagaries, weather
for its own sake is our great magician. The Dalesman may live
for a life-time under the same roof, and yet never weary of a land
whose face is for ever changing, for ever showing some new
wonder at the bidding of wind and sun and rain. From the
moors—turn any way you will, on a still, clear day—the
country stretches out and out, illimitable, sleepy and serene.
But go on a day when thunder brews and purple creeps downward from a sky of breathless foreboding, and you will see the
land for what it is. Great, shaggy hills stride over valleys, steep
gorges, shallow gashes. Purple lies in all these hollows, big or
little, and above their mystery the wan, green highlands show.
No acre of the Dale shows now as sleepy or secure. Storm to
come has brought its nakedness to view, and paints the wild
lands with a wizard's brush.

From these same moors, when dawn of an August day strides
ruddy up the mists, another country shows itself, though the
same hills guard the self-same valleys. The sun comes up, a
lusty groom, and draws the fleecy bridal gear away from rise and
hollow. The heather at your feet steams with warm incense of
its bloom. The larch-spinney at the edge of the broken fields
takes shape through the curling wreaths of mist. Nothing is
revealed in haste. It is as though you watched the world's
creation all afresh—a creation orderly, quiet, mystical. The
lower country gets slowly from its dreams and wakens to full
sunlight. No purple thunder-haze disguises the winding hollows. You can see their cosy farms, the sycamores that break

the storms for them. You catch the glint of purling streams, and hear the distant cawing of the rooks. And now the wonder of the day increases, step by step with the sun's up-coming. Far off across the lowlands, great belts of pine-wood glisten against a sea of crimson heather, and gaunt boulder-castles rear themselves, flecked with silver grey where mists still linger. All things are believable to-day—elves and fays and goblins on the moor about you—pixies in the silver threads of

It is as though you watched the world's creation all afresh

water dancing far below—ogres with two heads or twenty wielding dreadful cudgels, who live in the rock-castles. Then your own dreams go with the mists, and an ancient shepherd—curious, like all his kind—stands at your elbow. He has seen you long since, and stalked you with a carefulness unneeded. Beside him is a bob-tailed dog, all hair and suspicion and bright, clever eyes.

" Oh, it's a friend, is it ? " he said, with the smile worth a king's ransom.

" Near thereby, Ephraim."

" And you just stepped up to take a look at it all ? "

" Just that."

" You would. Sometimes I fancy you've been of the shepherd-folk yourself once, and can't forget it."

He lights a stump of a pipe that, judged by its antiquity, might have been dug out of some buried chieftain's grave in the mound behind us. He smokes in profitable silence, then looks out and over to the hills beyond.

" It's a new country every day—and yet, Lord bless it, it's the same."

No book of a thousand pages could tell our highland story as the shepherd does in that brief summing-up. A people of old longed always for some new thing—a thing without roots—a wind-flower dead at the moment it was plucked. The shepherd, lean and hard, great at the saving of ewes overblown in pitiless drifts, is rooted, age-deep, in the Dale. And the new face it shows to him each morning is of the sure yesterdays, leading to the hale to-morrows.

We sit on neighbouring boulders, with the bob-tailed dog between us, and listen to the harmonies of land and sky. He falls into talk of the grim, old fox that has his lair in the gorse thickets yonder below the moor—the fox that dines each day on chicken and eludes all traps and guns. He talks of life and death, of the stars that keep him company on night-time journeys, of foot-rot among sheep and the way to heal it—talks wisely, temperately, between slow puffs at his prehistoric pipe. Then the bees come winging up from lowland hives, till the heather-belfries are one low, droning chime. The native bees— " bigger and more bumblesome," as the shepherd puts it— get to their own work, too. And overhead the grey curlews sweep with infinite lament. One would have missed it all, if weather had not drawn one out of bed this morning to see what dawn was doing with the highlands.

There are the times of east wind, too. The east wind has few friends among the human sort. It has none elsewhere. Cattle and dogs and horses loathe it. Trees, budding untimely, wait till the tyranny is past. The very pastures shrink in dismay from the touch of its bitter passing. It comes unbidden and unwanted—comes from Siberian steppes, and over Europe's teeming, close-packed towns, and has no time to wash itself on the short journey overseas to our rough northland. It is good neither for man nor beast. It is sharp-toothed, venomous, barren of pity and hope. Yet it comes with the striding days of March, evangelist of lengthening days. Plover return from

The streams, where they wade deep, are dusky violet

alien haunts at east-wind time. The throstles get to a higher branch of leafless sycamores and fling out their wooing song. From the worst it can do to field and coppice, Spring's young challenge starts to birth. And the year grows to lustier man-hood, maybe, by grace of hardship at the start.

There's an old story in the Dale that, when the four winds went in search of fairy godmothers, three of them were blessed. The North wind would be strong and swift, a man; the South a soft and fragrant thing, his bride; and the West would bring them children bright with sea-foam on them from the distant coast. But the East had only a step-mother who drove him out of doors, a wanderer for all time and peevish with his wrongs. Yet this outlaw of the winds—against his desire, or with it—is a great painter of the hills. At no other time of year will you find the same eager lights, the like swift, never-ceasing play of colours that are gone before you capture half their beauty. Daffodil and rose, sapphire and green and purple, race westward over the grey fells. The streams, where they wade deep, are dusky violet; and the sheen of budding trees is all made up of red and copper hues, till one's eyes need rest from the bewilderment of field and moor and woodland.

Weather—" Dale's weather," as it is named by hard-tried affection—it is a great wayfarer to have for comrade.

XIX

A ROGUE OF SORTS

The Stranger—Kettlewell Sheep Fair—Selling a Watch.

WEATHER at times can bring its comedies. Once, when a casual autumn shower overtook me on the Kettlewell road, I sheltered under a wayside syca-more; and presently a little, smooth-stepping fellow joined me. He was neat and dapper, and carried a leather bag.

" Wettish," he said.

" Wettish," I agreed.

" Going to Kettlewell Sheep Fair, no doubt?"

" Yes, as it happens."

Nimble, inquisitive, with a clean-shaven, mobile face, the man puzzled me. Most of him was of the town, yet he seemed partly of the country, too, in some haphazard way.

" Buying?"

" No."

" Selling, then?"

" No."

" It's no manner of use to put me off," said the astonishing stranger. " I always ask questions on my way through this mixed vagabondage known as life. It pays to ask questions. Sometimes you learn a little, and sometimes a lot—and it all helps to keep the good pot boiling."

We of the country are reticent, most of us, by force of habit. I did not like the man. Clean and well-groomed to look at, soft of voice, there was a smell of oil about him, somehow. Speech and mind and body seemed smooth with a nether sort of subtlety.

"I'm going to the Sheep Fair, too," he went on, in answer to my stolid silence, "though I drive no ewes to market. All my stock-in-trade is in my bag here."

"Yes?"

"Oh, devil take your 'yes' and 'no'! D'ye own the Dale?"

"One little corner of it."

"Take to my trade, and you'll own the rest. It's the tongue of silver, and the heart that doesn't care a damn, that go merry all the way."

I was glad when the shower was over—glad that we were only a mile from Kettlewell, as he kept pace beside me, chattering ceaselessly. When we came to Kettlewell Bridge, and into the pasture on this side of it, he slipped away like a shadow-man, and I forgot him.

Kettlewell Sheep Fair was in progress—a fair in keeping with the grim, limestone crags that shield the narrow meadows and the pastures on either side Wharfe River. It is a gathering not to be missed by any lover of the Dale. The first glimpse of it is the story of bygone days that live on among us. Constant to types inbred by the generations, the thick-set farmers gather, and the wise sheep dogs, and the ewes bleating with a sorrow that will not be quiet. Above them are the ancient hills that know no changes, save of winter's cold and summer's heat. The men and the bleating ewes, the bright-eyed dogs, seem old as the hills, and as young.

The colouring of the scene is unforgettable on such a day as this. Grey-green fells, grey walls, russet bracken-slopes above; below, grey sheep and brown coats and gaiters of the buyers and the sellers; grey wood smoke from the clustered chimney-stacks, rising against sober russet of the trees—all is a blended harmony, and Wharfe herself—the river magical—glints russet-grey as she goes singing past. Most of the farmers you know, and many of their dogs. Everywhere is the ring of the true Dale speech, racy and unhurried. And one gaunt shepherd—come from the remotest uplands—is counting his sheep in terms of the old numerals. He is beyond praise or price, this shepherd, linking the dim past with modern stir

Kettlewell Sheep Fair

and bustle. From his far hill-cot he has brought the speech of an age incredibly remote, and with it the continuity that makes of the Dale a living, vibrant personality. Whatever changing times its folk encounter—alter the fashion of clothes and manners as the lowlands choose—ancient voices are about the hills to rouse heart-hidden memories of simpler forbears whose lives were given royally to fell-craft, to love of home and great knowledge of the poetry that thrives on lean mountain slopes.

A remembered voice breaks through the happy tumult.

" Who wants to know the time o' day ? "

The slippery rogue who sheltered with me under the sycamore is standing on a trestle table. Everything about the man suggests that in his time he has been an actor, playing in small theatres to little money. He begins to tell a droll story, drawing a knot of country folk about him. The art of his performance is excellent in its way. As the tale gains in humour, the sadness of his face deepens, till at the climax he is tragic to the point of abysmal gloom. A roar of laughter ripples up, and he dives into the bag beside him. The nut-ripe, mellow sunlight shines on a watch that seems to be pure silver.

" I wanted that laugh, friends. Now we're coming to business after a good beginning. Laugh, and the world laughs with you, as the poet says—grouse, and you grouse alone." He puts on an air of tragic gloom again, and earns his second roar of glee. Then he smiles on them, with a child's innocent frankness. " I have here, gentlemen of Wharfedale, a watch that all of you should own. You all *can* own one, for there are others in my bag. The sun that gets you up in the morning keeps no better time. In fact, it's a race between them, which shall be more punctual. Sometimes the sun wins, and sometimes the silver watch."

" Oh, cut the cackle, mister ! " growls a big farmer. " We're not such fools as the soft sort lower down the Dale."

" You're not. That's why I'm here. You've sense enough to know that this watch would be cheap at two pounds. Made in Switzerland, the earliest home of watch-making. Never tires, unless you come home market-dayish and forget to wind it."

" Meaning me ? " says the farmer aggressively.

" If the cap fits, friend, pursue such ways no longer."

His little world is certainly laughing now with the seller of watches.

"As I was saying," he goes on, "I sell at a loss when I ask only a pound for this priceless gem of the Geneva factories. I was ever a philanthropist. Sterling silver —the case alone worth what you give. Come, gentlemen, get busy. Who wants a watch? I can't stay here all day, waiting for you to snatch a bargain."

Tragedy returns to him when he finds nothing doing. He glances at the upturned faces with tearful grief.

"You want me to *give* them to you outright. Well, then, you see this envelope—and watch—and the pound I take from my own pocket. Watch and pound go into the envelope. Now, who buys?"

They know better, most of them, than to believe that something comes for nothing. Tillage of hard-won crops has taught them that. Then suddenly the swindle-merchant falls into soft, and purring talk, till by-and-by a hulking farm-lad begins to wilt. The vagabond senses him at once.

"That's the spirit," he says, with the most beguiling smile in Christendom. "There's a lass thinking of you somewhere, and she'll be bright and bonny when you show her a silver watch you bought for nothing."

The pound is handed up, and the envelope is handed down and the shock-headed lad goes apart with his bargain. He passes so close to me that I follow discreetly, curious to know how he will take the end of the affair—the certain end. He does not take it well at all. When the envelope discloses a watch only and no money, he stamps with bovine fury. Strange oaths frighten the still air, until he remembers the crowd not far away. With a cunning grin he  pretends to thrust the promised pound into his pocket, and retires to a distant corner of the field. He does not court close enquiry. The vagabond is engaged, meanwhile, in a chatty discourse on Switzerland and its hives of industry.

" The land of William Tell and of watches, gentlemen," he finishes. " A great country. Who is the next to give a pound for another silver timepiece, with his money given back ? "

Keenly as he glances about for another victim, he finds none. So he changes his tactics. In sorrow rather than in anger, he complains that they are not so shrewd as he had thought. If they wouldn't have a watch a-piece for nothing, he must ask ten shillings, and not a penny of it given back. Two purchasers respond at last to this proposition, and then trade grows slack once more.

" My heart aches, friends, when I think of the last time I was in Switzerland—the land of everlasting snow, and bows and arrows, and apples on boys' heads. There was a young girl— the only support of a widowed mother—busy watch-making. I bought all her stock. She would weep if she knew I was selling them for the beggarly price of ten shillings—or five, must it be ? Five shillings, then. I'd rather sell at a rank loss if by doing so I leave Kettlewell better for my coming."

" Go it, lad," mutters the big farmer who has kept his place stolidly. " Thou'st got the gab-gift, if naught else. But I don't believe in thee."

" You wouldn't. What you need is a watch that will lie to your wife when you come home on market-days. And I don't keep such in stock."

The sally sets a brisk five shilling trade going, and I leave him to it. Friends, from up-Dale and down, are scattered here and there about the field, and it is late when I get to the highway gate again. An altercation is in progress. My vagabond from the country of eternal snows and bows and arrows is confronted by his victim in the transaction of a pound returned for a pound, with a watch thrown in. The shock-headed laddie has his coat half off, and obviously his grievance has been rankling.

" I want a pound off you, and, by japes, I'm going to get it ! "

The vagabond is half his size, but shows no fear. With great dignity he appeals to the bystanders, as to a court of judge and jury met in solemn conclave.

" He took his luck of the game, and lost. What sort of sportsmen are you in the Dale ? "

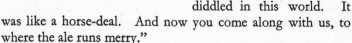

Solitude

They pondered the matter for a moment. Then they pushed the lad aside, and their spokesman laughed.

" Diddled him fair, you did—fair as ever I saw a lad diddled in this world. It was like a horse-deal. And now you come along with us, to where the ale runs merry."

That was the last I saw of him. I suspect that when they reached one of Kettlewell's hospitable taverns, he feigned to put liquor down his throat, as he had pretended to place money in an envelope. I am fairly sure that, keeping sober while they mellowed, he played the pound trick to good purpose. To the eternal snows of Switzerland he would add Greenland's icy mountains, no doubt, with a further hint of some Esquimau maid supporting her widowed mother by skill in watch-making. There was no limit to the wit of such a man. Memory of him fades as I take the homeward way. Dusk comes down, purpling the grey road. Strong silences gather from hills content with slumber, and the breeze plays like a kitten with early fallen leaves. Wharfe River flows softly through the gloaming with her evensong.

As one comes up Kirk Bank and through the enchanted woods of Netherside, a grey owl hoots across the road. A night-jar answers from the thickets. The spirit of the Dale keeps step with one along the highway.

XX

YOREDALE

NOWADAYS they name it Wensleydale ; but that, as the older folk have it, " is a soft, new-fangled notion." Its earlier title is Yoredale, and the cadence rings more true. Wensley itself is a village that might have been brought here from some southern shire in its entirety and planted in a sterner setting. Of its kind it is well-nigh perfect. Green, trim, gentle, it is a home for any shepherd's idyll, such as poets used to sing. The one note in keeping with the Dale is the ancient war-tattered banner in its church, with its arresting motto, *Aime Loyauté.* It is strange that in a village pledged to softness and repose a message so stirring should live on for the heartening of men; but Wensley, with all its charm, has no claim to give the Dale its title. Yore River, the stream whose infancy is guarded by the Dale's rugged heights, has that right. Yore is of the same breed as her sister, Wharfe, prone to spate and head-long passion between her gentler moods.

There are so many ways from one's own Dale over the tops to Yoredale that they constantly entice one to go gadding : steep, careless ways, all of them, striding through rocky lands that are friendly and sufficing in their harshness. One of the two most beguiling ways is the track from Kettlewell that leads into Coverdale—for itself, and because a legend disallowed by history tells how Christopher Norton, of Rylstone-in-Craven brought Scots Mary out of prison, and rode with her along these uplands : how he fought for her, too, where the little stone bridge ran crooked across the moorland beck : and how she watched him fight single-handed and prevail : and the way of their going together afterwards to his Rylstone house, where the Norton clan awaited them.

History affirms that Kit Norton rescued the Queen, but only for two breathless hours of flight on horseback that never came near the Wharfedale tops. But for me, whenever I go from

A Yoredale castle

Kettlewell to Coverdale, I have companions—Scots Mary, bonnie as a dream and tired to the heart of her, and young Kit Norton, soul and body on fire with the great adventure of his life. Her weariness is swept away. All her days she has known homage ; but this boy's clean, English fire is a poetry new to her. He is selfless in the enterprise, though she understands by every little token that he is wading deep in love. Such a boy, and so rare a man—to fight so well at grips with pursuit at the bridge— and now to be her courtier, as if she were of the stars, and he a man of earth—he has captured the Queen's imagination, if not her heart. The shadow of Fotheringay is already stealing round Stuart Mary. She knows herself captive to Elizabeth of England's jealousy and statecraft, knows that jealousy is the harshest of all gaolers.   But for her little while she is a pilgrim of the highlands, with free air and liberty about her—and beside her is this young hothead, glad to lose all in her cause if fortune wills it that way.

History frowns on the persistent legend that will always link this road to Coverdale with the Queen and Kit Norton ; but it affirms the truth of their escape from Castle Bolton.   The Castle, stout-walled and roofless, fronts you as you get down from Coverdale to Yore's lower reaches.   A great, thrusting pile of masonry, it dominates the valley, as who should say, " I watch all foemen come.   *Let them come*."   Behind it nestles the hamlet, trim, severe, well-kept.

Nothing could have shown Elizabeth's temper—its mixture of strategy and sheer relish of the ironic—more clearly than this choice of a prison for the Queen of Scots.   Scroope, the Governor of the Castle, was at once a staunch Catholic and a true believer in duty to whatever sovereign reigned in England. To put a man of his honesty and fine principle in the dilemma of guarding Scots Mary for a lengthy period was a master stroke. If he held her safe, so much the worse for his reputation with the Catholics.   If he connived at escape, there would be one less to trouble Elizabeth among the disaffected northern gentry.

There was in Elizabeth's mind, too, a petty and surprising under-thought that she would like to tempt Scroope, the simple-hearted lover of his wife.   Mary's compelling charm, effortless as the first break of spring when thrushes sing and cowslips nod, was known to all.   Well, let Scroope make what he would of it. If Mary could cozen worship from every man about her court in the hey-day of her queenship, what would her power be, when she was weak and tearful and a prisoner ?   Elizabeth understood men with an uncanny thoroughness, and had given peculiar care to her study of Scroope.   He had never been for self-advancement, like most of the men about her court.

Modest, self-reliant, resolute in action, tender and delicate in conscience, he was just the man to yield to Mary's charm in helplessness.

We know, from letters of the period, that Scroope did pass through a time of bitter travail. Elizabeth had gauged to a nicety the temptation, but not his strength to counter it. The faith he shared with his prisoner, his instinct to succour all

Nestles the hamlet, trim, severe

distress, for pity's generous sake—and with him, day by day, a lady so forlorn that her beauty gathered added charm—there could be only one end to the venture, as the English Queen pictured it. Scroope would let his prisoner go, and one gentleman the less would be at large in Yorkshire, the turbulent and reckless.

Scroope's handling of the matter was revealed suddenly, unexpectedly, on a fortunate day that brought me to Castle Bolton just as a grey but nimble stranger was coming, too, into the village. We exchanged greetings, country fashion, and he asked if I were a stranger to the neighbourhood. In that case he would put what little knowledge he had of the Castle at my service. I let him think me a newcomer, for something in his air suggested great eagerness to unfasten his pedlar's pack of story. His " little knowledge " proved to be a well of unplumbed depth. The Castle, stone by stone, was familiar to him with an intimacy precise and yet imaginative. He had strange tales of war and love and intrigue, played out here all in the olden days ; and he made dead folk live again with a sorcery complete. We were in tune together, and I told him how, all the way from Coverdale, I had been thinking of Mary Stuart and Norton's son from Rylstone, and how waywardly I longed for the story of their gallop over-tops to be true, after all. And then, in a twinkling, the man was changed. He could speak of something nearer his heart than I had sounded yet.

" I wish it had been true ; but they never got as far, except in dreams." Then he fell silent, till presently his keen glance roved about me, and seemed content. " So you're of the Queen's lovers ? Well, you're one of a biggish company. There'll never be her like again."

All this while we had been standing outside the Castle walls. Now he beckoned me within ; and, though the rooms were roofless to the sky, his hat was doffed. Here the Queen worshipped, in the ruined private chapel. And this was her withdrawing room. Since world's beginning there had been no queen but one for this alert and fiery poet of a man. He was vibrant in his joy.

" And this was the dining-hall. I will tell you what happened here."

So he, too, knew the footnote to Froude's history of the period—knew Christopher Norton's own description of the scene when, as far back as the year of Grace, 1570, he stood his trial for High Treason. I said nothing. To disturb this mood of my guide's was to jar a skilled painter when his soul was in the brush he plied.

" You will see a log-fire on the hearth.   Beside it the Queen is winding wool, and young Kit Norton holds the skein.   Scroope's wife, and many gentlemen of the household, stand about the room.   The table is already spread for supper, and the serving-maids all gone to bring it in.   At the far corner Scroope and Sir Francis Knollys are playing chess."

Yore's lower reaches

One cannot help but see it all.   The scene leaps vivid from his vision to one's own.

" Sir Francis glances up from the chess-board, after winning his game of chess, and sees the two by the hearth.   He calls the Captain of the Guard to him, and whispers privily to ask if Kit Norton ever keeps the Watch.   ' Sometimes,' said the Captain. ' Then see that he watches no more,' snaps Sir Francis.   So they changed the guard—but not Kit Norton's purpose."

To the rapt-away interpreter of a scene that lived and glowed, its poetry was part of his daily bread—the most essential part—but to me it was a quiet miracle, this living in the past.

" Think of it," he went on. " For twenty years they had the Queen in prison. For twenty years nobles and commoners were planning every way of rescue. And in all that time there was not one could do it, save Kit Norton. His plan miscarried for awhile ; but one morning the Queen walked down to the wicket-gate below the Castle, and found Kit there, with a led horse. He mounted the Queen, and they galloped."

The greybeard was a colt at play, listening to the hoof-beats of horses that had taken the road once with the only queen for him. The music was in his pulses. He had thrown off half his seventy years as he talked.

" For two packed hours of freedom they rode, and I've wished often I'd been Kit Norton that day. To do what no man else, before or after, had done for Stuart Mary—to have her for his own, just for the length of a two hours' gallop—there'd be enough to last a lifetime in such a memory."

When we left Castle Bolton, it was to follow the track taken by those old-time fugitives, and to stand at a certain spot on Leyburn Shawl where the Queen was recaptured—another milestone on the heartache road to Fotheringay. And from the Shawl we drifted quietly down to Leyburn, a brave market-town with a character all its own. One of the lasting joys of a free country life is this communion with fellow vagabonds. The chances of luck in the game are endless ; but there comes seldom such a red-letter day as this I happened on in Yoredale. My surprising comrade told me, with modest pride, that he had been given the charge of repairs lately done to the Castle. No restoration was aimed at, but simply strengthening of weak places lest ruin spread beyond the picturesque.

" I wasn't a mason," he explained ; " but they knew how I loved the old place, and understood its stones."

Nothing can describe the tone of those three words. I heard it once—just the same affectionate, quiet cadence—when I found a neighbour doing something contrary to all accepted garden-lore. He was transplanting things at the wrong time, or some backsliding of that sort, and I rallied him about the crime.

" Never you interfere betwixt man and wife," he said, with a solemn wag of the head ; " and specially never interfere 'twixt a man and his garden. This lile plot o' mine knows me, and I know her."

These are the men, one finds constantly, who achieve. They work by deep, romantic knowledge of their craft, and their methods necessarily astonish brethren of a weaker faith.

We came to a little shop-front, this Stuart lover and myself, that looked out on Leyburn's market-square. We went in ; and the great adventure was with us still.

" I'm only a simple trader, after all," he chuckled. " Small fry enough to be in love with Mary the Queen."

The man was irresistible. If he chanced to be a farm-hind tossing manure from the byres to ripen meadow crops, he'd build poetry from it—would see buttercups making cloth of gold above those meadows when east wind changed to west and spring set her young, eager feet about the land. What a shop it was. There was nothing here that had not lineage : Toby jugs, many coloured as Joseph's coat, neighboured teacups wide and delicate, blue-patterned. There were snuff-boxes, polished with such devotion that old voices lived again within them and bade you " take a pinch with me, sir." Tall grand-father clocks ticked solemnly. Their makers' names were long since part of England's history. Prior of Skipton, Snow of Pateley, Masram and Sager, and many another vouched for sound workmanship. Some of these clocks, in their owner's racy speech, " are slim as a lady, while other-some are buxom as a jolly farm wife." Each pendulum, gravely tick-tacking, had its own note, and their voices mingled with odd, beguiling harmony.

This antiquary cherished his clocks, his delf and china ware, as a born gardener loves his plants. His hands were tender with the fox-mask stirrup cups that once on a day were passed up to hunters when they gathered for the meet. There were swords stained crimson long ago on Marston Moor, and these he would not sell to any bidder at any price. What he left unsaid made so much plain. One room was given over entirely to Chippendale's craft in wood. Chippendale was born in a Wharfedale market-town; and none but a Dalesman, explained my host, could have learned just that way of handling wood. He had grown from babyhood in company with great boled elms and oaks. Trees had talked to him of their long growth, of the steadfast years kept safe against storm and tempest. And so, when their time came to be felled for men's uses, Chippendale sorrowed greatly for their death, till the wood came into his hands for making chairs, and he understood how eager and alive these old trees were. It was a revelation to him, and the wood he handled taught him how to use it, lest men forgot its ancient ancestry.

Again he said so little, this high priest among the antiquaries. Little by little we had come together in that mood when speech dwindles and true communion begins. The hour and the place, for once, were well met. He forgot almost that he had a listener —talked to me, gently, soberly, as his heart spoke, I fancy, when he was alone with his treasures, all Leyburn Town gone to bed, and he with his lamp, moving from one loved bit of merchandise to its cherished neighbour.

XXI

STUARTRY IN THE FIVE DALES

The 'Forty-Five—Dale Music—A Ducal Dominie—The Ghostly Pipers—Legends of Prince Charles Edward—The Retreat from Derby.

IN an old house, between the heather and the broken lands, the farmer opened his heart to me once about past days. His forbears had come across Solway Water, he told me, "twice in war against the English, and the third time in peace." And the story, unfolding slowly, brought romance—eager, young romance—into the hearth-place where we sat and smoked together.

The first time of their coming was in moss-trooping days, when one of his name "happed over the Border" with his fellows and took out of Westmorland great booty of cattle, ewes, and women. The spoil was named in this simple order, and gives a grimly humorous picture of relative values at that day.

The second time an ancestor of his crossed Solway was in 1745. He came with Prince Charles Edward, got as far south as Derby, and returned in the needless retreat that broke the Prince's heart. Through the Midlands the army came, and up among the Yorkshire Dales, and so across the Border, till the dull, sick winter marches brought them at last to Culloden and what happened there.

The third time of his family's crossing Solway was when this same ancestor, after Culloden, took to hidden glens and bye-

ways—the Highlands thick with soldiery in search of fugitives—
and worked his way slowly south. Then even the Scottish
lowlands, and Cumberland, and Westmorland, grew unsafe;
and he remembered how, on the retreat from Derby, he had lain
with a festering wound for two days and nights at a hospitable
farm in Wharfedale before taking the road again to join the
Prince's army. Perhaps, too, he remembered the yeoman's
daughter whose eyes had been bright and kindly. At any rate,

An old house, between the heather and the broken lands

when at last he reached the farm, and recovered after lying for
weeks between death and life, he stayed on, married the " Nut-
brown Nell," bonniest of the maids in a Dale famed always for its
women's beauty, and turned to the farm-work that was second
nature. Storm of the 'Forty-Five blew by. The fat, ox-like
prosperity of England browsed among lush grasses, and chewed
the cud, and slept. It had forgotten Crecy and Agincourt—
remembered no longer that Drake and Frobisher and Howard
had been sea-lords of the Main—accounted as little, because
it failed, the forward march to Derby, and the more amazing
retreat in good order.

That brief campaign emerges from the test of history as a gallant and a well-planned enterprise. It failed, not by its leader's fault, nor his soldiery's, but from the jealousy of a few chieftains who wrecked the enterprise. The farmer, who had never read a book in his life—he was unlettered—knew all this. He gave me snatches of the hot discussions in the Derby council chamber— told how the Prince was passionate for advance to London, how the Duke of Perth was eloquent for attack, and how, when sullen Murray and his sort threatened to withdraw their clans if foolhardiness went further, the Prince railed at them in a storm of heart-sick fury. All that I listened to, beside the quiet farm hearth, was true, as detailed memoirs of the time preserve the tale of Derby's council chamber. And there are details, passed down by word of mouth, that are unknown to printed history—little, intimate touches ringing true and rounding off the tale.

The Dales have many kinds of music, good to hear. Moor birds choir them with wild litanies—curlew, and redshank, and plover, roaming free spaces on pinions unfettered as the wind. Ousel-cock and thrush make melody when lowland meadows begin to put on their spring array. There's the storm's melody, too, when it dins about the naked highlands and the flooded glens. And there is the call of upland shepherds to their dogs, when it filters down the slopes in broken, rippling cadences. Quieter than all these, but vibrant with a hidden strength, is the music of tradition, heard by country hearths when you have learned the way of fellowship. To sit in a moorland farmstead and hear how it went at Derby when the 'Forty-Five was up, is to be aware of Stuartry, somehow, with a poignant joy that is akin to tears.

We had what seemed a commonplace farewell that day, the farmer and I.

" D'ye know Aysgarth and Mr. Drummond ? " he asked.

"I know Aysgarth. But who's Mr. Drummond?"

"Tell him I sent you, when you're next that way," chuckled my host. "Speak of the 'Forty-Five. You'll be surprised, I fancy."

The weeks went by after that, filled with one thing and another; but my chance came at last. What a day it was! From start to finish, one of those days when everything's in tune, and the world is all to rights. Up through Buckden the track led, and past lone Cray hamlet, and over into Bishopdale, where a blue sky shone on teeming hedgerow growth of briar rose and honeysuckle. Forward it wound through West Burton, rich in peace and garden-spaces all abloom, and on to Aysgarth. A flock of children came careering from the village school and out into the road in front of me; and they were followed presently by a grave, elderly man whose step was tired but full of curious dignity. All the way over and down I had been thinking of my quest, and nobody else was at hand to guide me. So I hailed the stranger, asking where Mr. Drummond was to be found.

"*I* am Mr. Drummond, sir—entirely at your service, if you need me."

The man's whole bearing was of another century, instinct with guarded courtesy. When I explained who had bidden me seek him out and talk of the 'Forty-Five, the grey wrinkles dwindled from his face. Alert and eager, he bowed me into his cottage, pressed hospitality on me, and then unlocked his tongue. Few came to his door who remembered the 'Forty-Five as anything but a far-off affair, foredoomed to failure and led by a stage figure known as Bonnie Prince Charlie. It was obvious that years of brooding silence were broken, now he had a listener who knew, at least, how little pageantry attended the bleak march south and north again through wintry Dales.

The story of his ancestor's coming into Yoredale, in every

detail almost, was that of the farmer who had sent me here in search of Drummond. He had gone sick during the shelterless retreat, had been succoured by a yeoman and his household, here in Aysgarth. Scarcely fit to take the road, he had followed and overtaken the main body of the army, to share Culloden later on. He had returned, a fugitive, to the Yoredale farmstead, had married the daughter of the house, and settled there. The outstanding difference between the two tales was that Drummond's forbear had found great difficulty in tackling farm-labour. He was unused to toil of this sort, and "framed unhandily" till he learned the way of tillage and the scythe.

"Does the name of Drummond carry no meaning to you?" asked my host, with a sober twinkle in his eyes.

I told him, yes. In the long ago there had been a Drummond, Duke of Perth, who was the Prince's trusted friend.

"He was my great-grandfather," said the village dominie—"and I'd be Duke of Perth, if the Stuart had happened over the water again, to come into his own."

Such moments seem to border on the miraculous. It is not possible to forget the delight, keen and tempered as a Ferrara rapier, that possessed me as I sat in this cottage and watched ancient loyalty play about John Drummond's eager face. He was young and alert again. And then he talked of the Great Adventure—talked as if he had ridden on it from start to hapless end. He made me hear the pipers as they played Royal Charlie into Edinburgh after Prestonpans was fought and won. I could see the court at Holyrood, with the Stuart hopes at flood and all the loyal city gathered for the ball. If the farmer who sent me here to find "Mr. Drummond" had lore of the campaign to give, it was of small account, measured by the storied garden of Drummond's mind and heart. The dominie had done with teaching children for a livelihood. He was among the shrines where his true life found strength and joy; and the privilege to hear him talk was mine.

From Edinburgh, when the only Ball of this adventure ended —ladies kissing hands, and what not—he led me south through winter snows. Through Cumberland and Westmorland we went, meeting bitter sleet on Shap Fell, where the lean lands rake to the sky. John Drummond was out of the body now, his whole being rapt away to the march on London. He seemed not to speak of matters passed down to him by hearsay, but to be there —there, where they happened. And when at last he came to Culloden Moor, and all that chanced among the heather on an

Where the lean lands rake to the sky

April day, this cottage was full of clamour. Battle, vehement and dour, surged between its walls. Carnage of fair fight groaned and cried in mortal anguish. Then came that other nameless carnage—killing of wounded Highlanders where they lay—and the sound of it crept naked and ashamed, seeking shelter from its own affright.

And then John Drummond put another spell on me. I saw Culloden when the dusk got down about the moor on that blood-drenched April day, heard men die of wounds that the night-winds nipped. All was negation, terror, uselessness, till the pipers came. Low and urgent, the wonder-music gathered strength. Urgent and sorrowful, it tarried awhile by the dead, then led one's spirit forward to other battlefields, to sorrow of wives and sweethearts who had long since gone to join their men. It was " The Flowers of the Forest " these ghostly pipers played. Born of Flodden's agony, the air had learned, centuries before Culloden, how to pluck poetry from hardship—the marching poetry that goes on blistered feet, forgetting pain. And John Drummond, glancing at me across the hearth, was himself the incarnate spirit of the 'Forty-Five. Triumph and despair, lament and bitter grief, joy of a sacrifice worth while— these were written in his face, plain for the reading.

*　　　*　　　*　　　*　　　*　　　*

It is odd how constantly zeal in any cause is served by what seems chance. Within three days of my meeting with John Drummond, I was flung suddenly into another Stuart venture, and that within a mile of my own door. It all happened because I wanted a Queen Anne teapot, and had asked a neighbour, skilled in the game of auctions, to get it for me at a local sale. When I went down to claim the treasure trove, two hand-painted prints were on the wall. Both were of fine workmanship, and both seemed to have been taken from some sumptuous volume of bird-lore such as graced the libraries of country gentlemen when the eighteenth century was at virile flood. The second print showed a kingfisher on a rock, with a half-eaten fish under its foot. Bold and simple in design, the thing attracted me so much that I nearly missed something written in clear, thin handwriting, on its upper margin: "*C.P.R. et C.G!* 1752." That was all; but it opened out a vista of sheer astonishment, of restless, eager query. My neighbour broke the silence.

" We've wondered a lot, the wife and I, about that Canadian Pacific Railway."

I bade him wonder no more, as there were no railways in those days.

" What does it mean, then ? "

" Charles, Prince Regent for his father, James the Third, exiled overseas."

What made me sure of my interpretation was the *C.G!* that followed, linked by the French *et*. It stood for *Commandant-Général*, in token that the Prince was in supreme command of any forces he could raise in Britain.

The mystery of that inscription, still unsolved, returns to one over and over again. The print itself was purchased in the most unlikely place—a village shop-of-all-sorts that sold chiefly brandy-balls and muffins. The old dame who sold it did not know how it came into her father's possession. The only house in the Dale that suggests itself as the first home of the print is Oughtershaw, where Wharfe takes her first infant steps. The Basil Woodd family was ever loyal to the Stuart; and often the picture comes to me of a room in the Hall there. It is a wet afternoon, some time in 1752, and one of the house takes down a great tome from the library shelf, and turns over its coloured bird-prints listlessly. Then suddenly he comes to the kingfisher, and interest is quickened. The kingfisher stands for the Stuart, the half devoured fish for Hanover; and hope of what still may chance bids him write " *C.P.R.*" in exquisite, clean penmanship. It is another way of passing the wine-cup over the water, to pledge the king across the seas.

An explanation, more alluring still, pleads insistently for hearing. It is fairly sure that the Prince was in England more than once in the troubled years that followed Culloden. Intent on another rising, he would waste no time in lukewarm London, but get up into the northern Dales on his way to the Highlands that had answered his first call so royally. It may be that Charles Edward, and no less a personage, was marooned by rain in that library at Oughtershaw. It may be that his own capable, firm hand wrote the message that has found one devotee at least to understand it in these later days.

How loyal to the Stuart was the family at Oughtershaw may be gauged by the history of those last moments when Charles the First stepped from an upper window in Whitehall to face the end with courage and great kingliness. Only three men were privileged to share the fine adventure—Bishop Juxon, Captain Basil Woodd, and Sir Thomas Sutcliffe. To Sir Thomas he gave, in his farewell words, the right to the crest his family cherished and passed down the centuries. To Basil Woodd he handed the jewelled star from his breast. That, too, the

A company of Prince Charles's men sheltered in a cave bordering the Malham Road

descendants keep to this day, as they hold to their hill-girdled home at Oughtershaw.

These Stuart episodes, legendary in the Dales, have all the charm of hill-mists. Grey, impenetrable, a sudden gust will open through the mists a corner of the highlands to you—a far-off crag, or a waste of bracken, golden-wet in the brief sun glow —and you know the homeland is about you, though it seemed lost and swallowed up a moment since.

At Skirethorns, near Linton-in-Craven, there is a persistent folk tale that a company of Prince Charles's men sheltered for the night in a cave bordering the Malham Road. In Yoredale a village dominie opens his heart, and you find yourself chatting, as it were, with the Duke of Perth. Again the mists are riven apart, and legend tells of Stuartry high up the fells of Amerdale. A lady of quality was riding home alone, at noon of a bleak winter's day, and encountered a band of wild men in tartan petticoats who surrounded her. They were fearsome enough to see, with their claymores and their kilts blowing tattered to the winds. The lady of quality counted herself lost beyond hope, till one of their number, " who had the English," approached her with grave courtesy. He then asked if she had seen any Georgian soldiery in the neighbourhood.

" Are you of the Prince's army ? " she asked, with a sudden lightening of the heart. " A kinsman of my own is with it."

She gave her name then, and the Highland officer had news that, when last he saw her kinsman, he was riding near the Prince as he pushed northward. She pressed them to accept whatever shelter her own house could offer them; but he checked her eagerness with the grave, quiet courtesy that had come to flower along these bleak highlands of retreat.

" There's no need to bring peril on our well-wishers."

With that he kissed her hand, and led his tattered Highlanders up-fell into the grey, sullen mists that seemed a funeral-pall for all that died in Derby Town when Murray played step-father to the 'Forty-Five. And she watched them go, with a melting of the heart and a rush of tears. They were so like her kinsman, side by side with the Prince somewhere on the northern road.

The mists close again about that legend, too ; but the rift has shown another glimpse of Dales history that links us to the 'Forty-Five. I have known men come into our highlands for the fishing and shooting, or because they knew them rich in limestone flora. Maybe they came in search of British camps and Roman roads. But they have stayed, giving up all else in the blandishment of finding here and there, in widely separate places, authentic history of Britain's last forlorn hope—the greatest of them all since Hereward, last of the English, held the marshlands against Norman William. They soon realize that pursuit of Stuart story is no easy pastime, and they come long after dalliance of summer with the glens is over. They take the wind-driven tracks known to men of the Retreat. You shall not learn what Stuartry has to tell, except on such journeys and in weather that tries you as it tested way-worn men who trod the road before your time. Name it a pilgrimage, if you will.

They find, these pilgrims, that hearts are opened to them—not doors only—in unexpected places. If one is single-hearted for the Stuart quest, it is known by many tokens. The travellers may halt at a long farm near Muker, where Swaledale gets up into the naked screes and the ravens are not altogether banished yet. His welcome may be ill assured, from the kennelled dog at the door to the farm-wife who answers his knocking. Then, the pass-word given, he is indoors, the house at his command, and presently the goodman gets to his feet, and goes upstairs, and returns with a claymore and a dirk.

" There's Culloden blood on them," says he, with grim and ancient pride.

Everywhere, in these hill-land outposts that sentry memories of the 'Forty-Five, there's the same tenacity, the unyielding homage to a cause lost long ago, but victorious still. The Stuart pilgrim, here in the North, learns from the men whose ancestors shared it of what stuff the 'Forty-Five was made— learns it in close, intimate detail. It is time the story was retold, before its stern reality is lost utterly in the mists that hinder true romance. Bonnie Prince Charlie, kilted and the King of Hearts, dances at Holyrood. The women jostle each other to kiss his hand. Thenceforth for ever he is pictured as a stage figure, adored for skill in pageantry.

We in the Dales have another view of Prince Charles Edward. We see a simple gentleman of fortune embarking in a tiny ship on the French shore. He has four comrades with him. The sloop pushes her way through mixed weather to the west coast of Scotland. The company disembarks. Five men have landed, to rouse Britain to the old allegiance. Pluck without faith avails little. Faith avails little, unless courage serves it. These five had both. The venture was incredible, if it had not happened. The five, led by Charles Edward, went up and down the Isles. The Highlanders' long dreams were answered. The Stuart was among them once again. Nothing mattered, now the lean years were ended.

They gathered to him, little companies of men born to combat and the Stuart glamour. Their boats pushed presently to the mainland, and loyalty swept like a heather fire from glen to glen. And always with them was the Stuart of their dreams, a youngster who knew when to be grave and when to jest—a prince who came to light their ancient beacons. Not all the chieftains he had hoped for joined his cause. Recruits from the Lowlands came scantily, though by that time there was the victory of Prestonpans to spur the laggards on. When they crossed the Border and went by forced marches south, disappointment found its keenest edge ; for the English rallied in slender numbers to the standard. Lancashire, old in Stuart zeal, remembered the earlier 'Fifteen, with its disastrous muddlement, and held aloof —most of the county—from all but sympathy.

In spite of disillusion, the little, compact army held its course towards London and the Throne. Two armies were on its flanks by this time, in hot pursuit, but could never catch it up. Through grim weather and a hostile country the Prince led his men till at last they won to Derby. News met them there that twenty thousand troops were guarding the approach to London. My Lord Murray wrecked the whole enterprise at this stage. Always jealous of the Prince's generalship, he pitted the dour arithmetic of warfare against the genius that inspired and could have carried through the forlornest hope that ever kindled England's story. There were two armies close behind, said Murray, and now they had news of a third in front of them. It was madness to go forward.

Murray had his way. He was to learn afterwards that the army at Finchley was notoriously rotten, that the King it was supposed to guard was already packing his valuables in readiness for flight to his home-country overseas. There is no need to dwell on the appalling grief that shook Charles Edward, as with ague, when the Council went against him. He was sure of his Highlanders, sure that they had only to press forward to find London theirs.

At dawn of the next day the Highland soldiery, obedient to their chieftains, marched north through Derby's streets. There was a wan moon struggling with wet, wintry sunlight. Sleet lay on the sleeping house-roofs, and a quiet sobbing ran along the ranks of bearded Highlanders who knew how to fight but were unskilled in battles that were lost before a blow was struck.

There is need—insistent need—to tell how Charles Edward took this changed adventure. All that had once been Prince Rupert—full-blooded for the charge, headlong for kingship and romance, when Charles the First held rule—fired the blood of this younger Stuart. As Charles Edward rode into Edinburgh after Prestonpans—alert, and proud, and happy—so he would have gone to London, his Highlanders behind him—would have ridden with gallant mercy for the conquered.

That dream was wrenched from him at Derby. Between one day's down-going and the next sunrise he had faced what few men are asked to meet, had fought it out in silence. When they brought his horse to him on the morrow of the Council, he declined it. The Duke of Perth, solicitous for his ease, pressed him unduly, and the Prince's temper broke.

"My Lord Murray leads, now we're in retreat. Go tell him so, with my prayers that he rides saddle-sore."

That gust of temper ended, the Prince took his place as rear-guard of the army he had led. Peril lay behind them now. Throughout the long retreat, Charles Edward had to go horsed at times; for Murray, who had fathered the turning-back, was already peevish with the child of his own begetting. Jealousy had lured him into dire mistake; and, knowing it, he grew to the likeness of a man gone mad. The chieftains who at Derby had been won by Murray's eloquence were ready now to dirk him.

The Prince rode among them, planning the details of retreat with surprising genius. They had fancied him a leader for victory only, and were amazed to find how patiently he arranged the thousand difficulties that beset this march of vanquished men. The country they traversed was bitter in hostility, all through the Midlands and the Yorkshire lowlands. The Highland chieftains were wild to pick quarrels with each other. Their soldiery were mad to run loose among a jeering populace that put shame on their Prince at every roadway bend.

Charles Edward stilled their riot, day by day and hour by hour. And constantly he got from saddle, and trudged up and down the ranks of foot-sore, limping soldiery. He had enticed these Royalists from far-off glens with promise that they would set a Stuart on the Throne again. He had failed them; and out of that failure grew a surprising strength and gentleness. The broken leader was one of them on this harsh, foot-sore business of retreat. If all that might have been gathered to the heart of an islander from Skye, and he fell sick of the trouble, the Prince was with him, telling him that he, too, understood the way of heartache. If a man's feet were blistered, Charles Edward knew the remedy, and found it in some wayside herb-garden as they passed by.   He was skilled in the lore of herbs.

The Prince's leadership of that grim foray down from Scotland, starry hope in front, would alone have made him one in history with Harry the Fifth—one with his kinsman, Rupert of the Rhine.   His leadership of the retreat gives him a place all his own, secure till history's memory grows dulled by age.   You may gather the tale from many books, published when friends and enemies of Charles Edward rushed busily into print after the 'Forty-Five was lost.   Zeal of well-wishers, rancour of foes,

The harsh, foot-sore business of retreat

show the Prince emerging constantly from the torture of defeat to find a greater courage, a swifter fellowship with way-lost men.

Dreams had gone down the sunset hills.   His one aim now was to get his army north, step by step, till onset of the last battle came.   His sole desire was to die, leading his men in a hope forlorn indeed by this time.   Moreover, he had a raging toothache that was fed by sleet-winds from the north ; and pain of this sort, counted slight and a small affair, nags courage from the hardiest man.   The Prince's feet, too, were road-sore from long trudging with his heart-sick infantry.   Intimate, crude details, these, but they serve to bring into sharper relief Charles Edward's utter desolation.   Heart and spirit and body—all were sick and maimed—and pride was roughly bruised. What was there to care for but the broken men who shared his desolation ?

Their march reached the Yorkshire Dales at last. The advance had been straight and orderly through Airedale, the army compact for victory. The retreat, when it came to the Five Dales, opening northward like the fingers of a hand, sent little companies straggling from the main route. Wharfedale knew many such. Nidderdale knew them, and hamlets washed by Yore and Swale. These stragglers were among hill-men now, who knew how to appraise quiet travail under hardship. They found a welcome denied them in the softer lowlands. Some, like John Drummond's ancestor, plodded north again to share Culloden's rout. Others, put out of action for weeks that denied all hope of overtaking the retreat, stayed on and married buxom daughters of the farms that gave them hospitality. That is why it is never safe for a stranger to the Dales to speak lightly of the Stuart. He may happen to disturb old memories that will settle on him as if he had disturbed a sleeping hive of bees. Years since, the Skye Boat Song met me round a corner of the road :

> " *Speed, bonnie boat, like a bird on the wing*
> *Over the sea to Skye.*"

I should have known who was coming, even if his queer-coloured dog had not preceded him. Nobody but Farmer Metcalfe, thickset and square to all the winds that blow, ever sings of Skye along our village roads. We passed, after the usual grim reference to Dale weather ; and I knew, but he did not, that an ancestor of his had heard the ballad once on the Misty Isle itself.

The rancour and corrosion of politics connected with the 'Forty-Five are long since stilled. There can never be another rising. Whatever bias men have towards one side or the other of that far-off strife, none need fear to yield homage to the simple gallantry that has outlived defeat. Defeat ? The memory of that lone marching north is remembered, as few victories are. Not only Highland eyes grow dim to-day in recollection, but English hearts are stirred by the epic of the 'Forty-Five. Perhaps our Dales bye-ways are given special leave to understand such matters. No wild joy of the marching south stirred their

Castle Bolton

pulses unduly, but the way of broken men, returning, moved them to their depths. The Dalesmen love battle with weather and crops hard to win. They love a healthy feud, as duellists revelled once in sword-craft. But most of all they warm to a forlorn hope bravely carried through to whatever end awaits it.

How can you miss the reality of encounters at some silent road corner ? No traffic stirs. Dusk of the long day's ending steals from moor and coppice. One's thoughts, if one is conscious of thought at all, are with the modern homeland. Then down the silence comes a thin and elfin music, gathering strength. The lament takes clearer meaning. The skirl of pipes has come from far-off Scottish hills to this our Yorkshire Dale. They will not be denied. Near they sound, and nearer, till all the road is quick with tramping feet, and all the night is vibrant with sorrow of the pipes. " The Flowers of the Forest " they are playing—a dirge for Flodden once, and now a dirge for the Prince's Scotsmen who fell by the way in the retreat from Derby—fell in our northern Dales.

Once every while they come from far Culloden Moor, these pipers, and revisit every grave where one of theirs died on English soil. They come down the long Dale of Wharfe, saluting their dead as they halt awhile, and then pass forward. And the heart melts in a man privileged to hear the Ghostly Pipers in such a pregnant hour. All that is Stuartry returns—the gallant, striding hope, the sick retreat—the further recompense awaiting Prince Charles Edward and his Highlanders when they had done with this world's muddy gawds.

XXII

A LAND OF SHEER DELIGHT

*The Skirfare—Arncliffe—Cosh—The Ancient Sheep Numerals—
Semerwater — Cray — Coniston — Hubberholme — Wharfe's Age-Old
Charm.*

WHARFE RIVER has a most beguiling tributary, the
Skirfare, that waters Amerdale. Not far beyond
storied Kilnsey, with its massive, Sphinx-like Crag, a
second track leaves the main highway and winds up into the naked
pasture-lands, and with it marches the joy of solitary spaces and
of friendly loneliness. You will hear no voices but of moor-
birds—redshank and jacksnipe, curlew and slant-wheeling
plover—and of bleating ewes.

Across the narrow valley Hawkswick nestles, orderly and
trim, beneath the limestone scarps. Spring's alternate cloud
and sun give the further hills a wild magic of their
own. And so one comes to Arncliffe, the little capital of
Amerdale. How grey she is, and old, and comely. Ancient
houses border the unspoiled village green. The Falcon Inn
stands as such a tavern should, unobtrusive in its simple dignity,
instinct with the hospitality of other days. Post office and farms,
cottages and bigger homesteads, are part of the one community,
watched over by great-boled trees that have forgotten their
birth-century.

This seems to be all the village, till you stray down the hill and
find yourself at the bridge that has few rivals in a country
renowned for its far-flung, graceful arches. A church, grey as

the bridge, stands on one side ; on the other is a little old house that seems to live in a fairy-tale come true. It is big enough for ease, small enough for comfort. Its windows look out on lawny garden ways that dip their feet into Skirfare's pleasant stream. Instinctively you picture a gentlewoman of the spacious days, living here in a house destined for her from the start of things.

Arncliffe

In sober fact, just such a gentlewoman did live in the house on the brink of Skirfare. Strong in spirit, instinct with charm and frolic tenderness, she has left an enduring legacy to a country that does not forget such personalities. Charles Kingsley, while he was questing through our northern highlands for the atmosphere that later on was to give us *The Water Babies*, found a welcome at Bridge House, here in Arncliffe. The influence of the house, its mistress and the peat-brown stream, is clearly to be traced in a book that survives through modern days. I know few houses in the five Dales of Yorkshire that are easier to stay with, harder to leave. Yet the track beyond is beguiling enough. It strays, uphill and down, to Litton, smaller than Arncliffe—to Halton Ghyll, smaller still—to tiny Foxup set among a wilderness of lean fields, boulders, hazel-scrub. Foxup would seem to be the loneliest outpost of Amerdale ; but there's a lonelier.

The first time I travelled the road to Cosh—if road it could be named—was in mid-winter snow. Soon after leaving Foxup the drifts lay piled to the wall-tops. Only a narrow space of track was cleared, winding endlessly, it seemed, into the wilderness above. No bird called. The wind was silent. All the land stretched dumb and empty to a leaden sky. Then a farm-dog barked noisily, and the relief was instant. Something was alive, after all, in this land that seemed to have lain dead for unnumbered ages. A sudden bend showed a hollow of the uplands, and in it stood a stout farmstead. Children were playing in the snow. A buxom farm-wife ran to the door, to learn what the dog's warning meant. The contrast was bewildering, between the loneliness that had been and this present, human warmth.

The second time I took the road was in June, the month that plies witchcraft in among the fells. Where snow had been, the waste was a garden strewn with flowers. Hoar rocks were afoam with primrose-bloom. Hyacinths made little, blue carpets under clumps of hazel scrub. Soft breezes roamed from a dappled sky, and all the birds were choiring summer up. It was only then, as I looked down on Cosh, that its singular, compelling charm grew clear. Its hollow was wider and deeper than our first, snow-bound acquaintance with one another had shown. There was room for a croft and garden between the guardian slopes where sheep were browsing in and out among the primrose-clumps.

There is no other farm like it in the Dales, and no other name. In Scandinavia the shepherds' huts, built high up the mountains, are named *Kosh*; but they are deserted when winter sets its teeth about the heights. The Norse breed in one Dalesman of old days bade him name this farmstead Cosh and gave him pluck to dwell there throughout what winter can do " when her weather-mood is in."

At Cosh, not very long ago, there was a farmer who remembered the ancient sheep-numerals, passed down by tradition. When he took his ewes to market, he could count in modern terms. On the heights he shed such frippery, and to be with him was to rejoice in the music of past days. *Een, teen, tethera, fethera, fip*—is that not a gallant way of rendering our prosaic one to five ? Through *obera, dobera* the counting goes, and on to *eendie, teendie, tetheradie*, and forward to the altered cadence of *eenabump, teenabump, tetherabump, fetherabump*. What is the ancestry of these numerals ? Few hazard even a guess ; but those who have heard them spoken suspect that they were taught upland shepherds by the wastes that fed their ewes. Out of rock and moor and scanty herbage they sprang, rude with the melody of wind-swept spaces. *Een, teen, tethera*—they get into your heart like a song as you leave Cosh behind and trust to such tracks as happen here and there for guidance through wild country. Rise after rise, the gaunt lands sweep and billow to the mountains' feet. The breeze is swift and merry. By-and-by the haphazard tracks lead down and up, only to dip and rise again, till unexpectedly the journey's end shows near. Deep in the cradle of the hills lies Semerwater, the lone, mysterious lake that lays its spell on casual wayfarers. Not only its situation, but its heart, is solitary. Two age-old hamlets border it, remnants, legend says, of a city that kept great pomp and revelry in the dim times of eld. William Watson yielded to the lure of Semerwater, drew inspiration from her brooding silence, and gave us the most shapely and alluring ballad of our modern times.

A proud castle stood here once, they say, and goodly dwellings. All was prosperous as a dream, till there came a night of bitter storm. The wind nipped shrewd to the bone. The rain was pitiless. Into the township came a man as ancient as his tattered clothes, asking bite and sup and a night's lodging. None gave it. They were too busy with prosperity and all it offered them of indoor ease. Who was this tattered fellow, to come troubling their ease? The wanderer came to the little farmstead at the township's end. It was his last throw of the dice against adversity. This time the door was not shut on him, but opened wider. They warmed him with spiced ale and food, gave him their bed to sleep in, while they drowsed by the hearth downstairs. All three slept sound that night.

Semerwater

They did not hear the flooding rains, the wind that roared in wild-beast fury. When they were astir again next day, all was quiet. The storm had gone to some further lair among the hills, and mellow sunlight bathed the land. This same sunlight showed them a blue, foam-flecked lake where the town once had been. Castle and proud dwellings and lesser houses lay deep and drowned under Semerwater. *Deep and drowned*. No other poet of our time could have captured that sure inspiration. Semerwater, to this day, is not as other lakes. To haunt its borders is to be held by an increasing spell. The natives say that on still, clear evenings you can still see broken roofs under the silent waters, and hear church-bells ring out a muffled peal.

Deep and drowned. That old description of the great, reed-girdled tarn suffices. Drowned in her own deep memories, brooding for ever under the desolate fells, she mourns for the city she once slew, and will not be comforted. The *Ballad of Semerwater* goes with you, long after you have left her margin and passed up the rutty track that leads, with many a turning, to the road known as the Stake. A brave road, that fears no climb. Sometimes it is bordered by lush wild-rose hedges, oftener by craggy limestone walls, till it brings you at long last into an authentic highway of the King's. Uphill, the road winds over into Bishopdale. Turning right-handed, you find yourself in a country of steep, plashing rills that gush with music from every crevice of the rocks. And so you come to Cray, its inn and single farmhouse perched solitary on the brink of a wooded, deep ravine.

To sleep in this inn is to awake next morning to a sense of spacious ease. The air blows sweet from the massive bulk of Buckden Pike ; and everywhere there is the roar and bubble of descending waters. Cray holds its own among all Wharfe's secluded corners, a hamlet instinct with peculiar charm. From the pasture-lands above the inn, where grey, stone fences stride to the further skies, you look down-dale on Buckden. Once the Cliffords' deer-forests stretched from Skipton to these heights—to Barden, too, and Langstrothdale. There is no herd now in all the country, except Miss Crompton-Stansfield's, at Buckden—a gallant herd, led by a stag known among us as " Hereward the Wake," because he still holds Buckden for the times that were. Beyond, out of sight, but not of memory, lie Kilnsey, and pleasant Coniston with the Maypole on its tiny green, and behind it the deep cleft that once brought floods down so stupendous that nothing was left of the village but its church and a neighbouring house or two on the hill. A small church, Coniston's, simple in design, but rich in the sense of worship which pervades all the Dale's six ancient fanes.

From this high outpost above Cray you come down by wooded tracks to another of Wharfe's swift ambushes. All the way up from Bolton Priory she has been leading you to Hubberholme, a hamlet so sequestered that time itself seems to pause here for memories of a past hoar with antiquity. Hubba the Dane raided, and fought, and harried, till he came to the end of his warfaring lust, and settled here at Hubberholme. They say it was he who built the first rude kirk, whose site is covered now by a church so comely in its grey old age that it brings a gust of sheer emotion to the wayfarer. It is incredibly ancient—not in its fabric only, but in the lusty faith that taught the masons how to build. Without and within, it is its simple self, rough-hewn. Shepherds from the hills came to share the work, one fancies, and strapping farmer-lads, and foresters from Buckden. They were not skilled with the chisel. None left his mason-mark on the stones he hewed. But all gave the heart-song that informed the hammer-taps, the eager faith that is instinct in its walls. In later days, when trouble came to the Percies in Northumberland, they sent their Rood Screen here to Hubberholme for sanctuary. Part of it still remains, mute witness to the lapse of centuries.

Neighbour to the church stands a curious and pleasant inn. It turns its back on the road. Its front looks out on stables that were busy once, when horses were the only fast means of traffic. Grace Pawson kept it in days that grow near in retrospect—a Daleswoman, bred true to type. Shrewd, quiet, witty when occasion served, she ruled her house and all chance-come travellers with a hand of steel hidden by a velvet glove.

From Hubberholme the Dale's enchantment grows. You go by way of a scarce-travelled road to Deepdale, with its bridge that seems old as the limestone fells and the climbing pastures—past Beggarman's, a solitary farmstead, its roomy house and outbuildings set in a ferny hollow among the naked grasslands. And beyond Beggarman's again you come to Oughtershaw, last outpost hamlet of the Dale, its old Hall linked inseparably with Stuart days by memories of Captain Basil Woodd.

The brook that waters Oughtershaw is still Wharfe River. Get up among the bouldered lands above, and you attend her birth, as she leaps from many a spring-fed cranny into the light of eager day. No river in the land has Wharfe's compelling personality. Here at her source, among the mountainous, wide spaces, with plover crying overhead and a thin breeze piping from the heights, you understand what trains her infant steps. Struggle of birth-time, as she emerges from lonely journeys underground, where the deep limestone caverns are, and unplumbed lakes lie cold and dark—joy of the sunlight and the merry breezes when she escapes from her many prison-houses—these go with her still as she runs through Oughtershaw, and down past Coniston to croon a slumber-song to the folk who sleep in Linton's tranquil churchyard.

Under the wooded heights of Lythe she runs—under Loup Scar, the gaunt rampart that once felt the tread of Tom Lee's feet, heard the sullen splash as the murderer threw his victim to the pool below—and on to the rounded sweep of waters which is instinct with sequestered peace. Past Burnsall kirk she journeys, and under grey arches of the bridge first reared by William Craven, that forthright lover of the Dale. Does Wharfe remember, when she flows by in tranquil sleep of summer, how often she got down from the snow-loosed heights to throw Burnsall Bridge like a plaything to the foamy madness of her waters?

Deep-hidden she goes under the grey, steep village known to the native-born as Aptrick, through a land of infinite beguilement, till she reaches Barden, the bridge of her heart, that only once fhe overthrew in her most headlong passion. They say that on still nights you can hear the clank of Clifford's men, as on the day they crossed to the battle known as Flodden Field—can sense the rhythm of their marching feet.

And now Wharfe glides pensive as a dream between lush woodlands. Poetry is in her song. Her banks are clustered thick with primroses. Grave, ancient trees return to youth's vanity, and take pleasure in their comeliness, mirrored in the slow-gliding stream. By-and-by a little fret gets up among the waters. Scuds of foam begin to ride them. They seem of small account, like cloudlets in a peaceful sky, till suddenly Wharfe glides down to a place of ambush. Still her surface is smooth, unruffled ; but under it lie caverns she has scooped from living rock, deeper and more drowned than Semerwater.

The whole river narrows to a man's long stride. Below, wide galleries let her waters through. All here is smooth, beguiling treachery. The Boy of Egremonde was checked in his leap by the hound he held in leash. Folk less picturesque are tempted constantly to the stride that calls, low and soft, with summons of the water-maidens. One hesitation, or wet rock underfoot as the leap is taken, and another goes to Wharfe's tally of her slain. And now again she broadens out in a repentant curve that embraces Bolton Priory with a living, tender arm. She recalls how many trout she gave aforetime for Friday, when the steadfast monks lived there, the foresters and waggoners and those who tended the red deer up the hills. And her song is all of betterment and praise.

Here, on the wild uplands above Oughtershaw, where Cam Beck is simply " The River," taking her first haphazard steps, one understands Wharfe's age-old charm. Headstrong, passionate, tender, full of baffling waywardness, she is so human, so strangely lovable and dear. Here, too, among the mountains' austere stillness, the heart finds breadth and liberty to recapture a lifetime's caring for Wharfe's Dale. And the best hour is when dawn of a blithe April day sends crimson fingers out across the mists, and the air is chill and sweet. The sun gets up, hale and lusty, strewing the mists into gauzy tatters. Peak after peak appears, fold after fold of the valleys whose every hearth—sending up lazy smoke by this time—is known to long acquaintance

No Dale gives unearned freedom of its borders to any man. He must win it, as other spurs are won, by adventure and by ceaseless constancy. Dawn and dusk, midwinter through the drifts, travail and joy of shepherds up the heights, ding of tempest and the sun's scorching heat—these must grow into his life before he knows the Dale and wins the inner caring that is weather-proof, secure.

A melody gets into one's heart, here on Cam Fell. It is good to have lived and known the amazing strength and beauty of lands watered by The River. Old years return, trusty cavaliers, beside one. There comes a clear, forthright picture of fell and mountain, of valleys burgeoning with spring's enchantment, of storied kirks and castles staunch for battle. Wharfe threads it all with her glamoured, ever-changing melody. She can make music out of harshest odds, or sing quiet songs of faëry.

The River will be with us as we near the Further Brink, will choir us over the last Brigg of all. That is the Dalesman's faith, hard-won and eager.

INDEX

INDEX

INDEX

Printed in Great Britain by Butler & Tanner Ltd., Frome and London
945.1138